D0917165

3 6021 00085 6249

Developing Self-Regulated Learners

Beyond Achievement to Self-Efficacy

NO LONGER
PROPERTY OF
JEFFERSON
COLLEGE
LIBRARY

Jefferson College Library
Hillsboro, MO 63050

PSYCHOLOGY IN THE CLASSROOM: A SERIES ON APPLIED EDUCATIONAL PSYCHOLOGY

A collaborative project of APA Division 15 (Educational Psychology) and APA Books.

Barbara L. McCombs and Sharon McNeely, Series Editors

Advisory Board

Sylvia Seidel, National Education Association

Debbie Walsh, Chicago Teachers Union, American Federation
 of Teachers

Ron Brandt, Executive Editor, Association for Supervision and
 Curriculum Development

Isadore Newton, University of Akron

Merlin Wittrock, University of California, Los Angeles

David Berliner, Arizona State University

Noreen Webb, University of California, Los Angeles

Series Titles

*Becoming Reflective Students and Teachers With Portfolios
 and Authentic Assessment*—Paris & Ayres

*Creating Responsible Learners: The Role of a Positive Classroom
 Environment*—Ridley & Walthers

Developing Self-Regulated Learners: Beyond Achievement to Self-Efficacy—
 Zimmerman, Bonner, & Kovach

Inventive Strategies for Teaching Mathematics—Middleton & Goepfert

Motivating Hard to Reach Students—McCombs & Pope

*New Approaches to Literacy: Helping Students Develop Reading
 and Writing Skills*—Marzano & Paynter

*Overcoming Student Failure: Changing Motives and Incentives
 for Learning*—Covington & Teel

Teaching for Thinking—Sternberg & Spear–Swerling

In Preparation

Designing Integrated Curricula—Jones, Rasmussen, & Lindberg

Effective Learning and Study Strategies—Weinstein & Hume

Positive Affective Climates—Mills & Timm

Dealing With Anxiety in the School—Tobias & Tobias

Developing Self-Regulated Learners

Beyond Achievement to Self-Efficacy

Barry J. Zimmerman, Sebastian Bonner, and Robert Kovach

The Graduate School and University Center
The City University of New York

AMERICAN PSYCHOLOGICAL ASSOCIATION | WASHINGTON, DC

Copyright © 1996 by the American Psychological Association. All rights reserved. Except as permitted under the United States Copyright Act of 1976, no part of this publication may be reproduced or distributed in any form or by any means, or stored in a database or retrieval system, without the prior written permission of the publisher.

Published by
American Psychological Association
750 First Street, NE
Washington, DC 20002

Copies may be ordered from
APA Order Department
P.O. Box 2710
Hyattsville, MD 20784

In the UK and Europe, copies may be ordered from
American Psychological Association
3 Henrietta Street
Covent Garden, London
WC2E 8LU England

Typeset in Berkeley and Bell Gothic by University Graphics, Inc., York, PA
Printer: Data Reproductions Corporation, Rochester Hills, MI
Cover Designer: KINETIK Communication Graphics, Inc., Washington, DC
Technical/Production Editor: Edward B. Meidenbauer

Library of Congress Cataloging-in-Publication Data
Zimmerman, Barry J.
    Developing self-regulated learners: Beyond achievement to self-
    efficacy / Barry J. Zimmerman, Sebastian Bonner, and Robert Kovach.
        p.   cm. — (Psychology in the classroom)
    Includes bibliographical references.
    ISBN 1-55798-392-5 (pbk.   :   alk. paper)
    1. Learning   2. Self-control.   3. Study skills.   4. Academic
achievement.   I. Bonner, Sebastian.   II. Kovach, Robert.
III. Title.   IV. Series.
LB1060.Z56   1996
370. 15'23—dc20   96-32053
                                                              CIP

British Library Cataloguing-in-Publication Data
A CIP record is available from the British Library.

Printed in the United States of America
First Edition

TABLE OF CONTENTS

PREFACE

> If you give a man a fish, you feed him for
> a day
>
> If you teach a man to fish, you feed him
> for a lifetime
>
> Confucius (551–479 B.C.)

We believe that all students have the power to become "smart learners" if they use self-regulatory processes to study more effectively. Each of us came to this conclusion from compelling personal experience as learners, teachers, and researchers. Barry J. Zimmerman is an educational psychologist who for more than 25 years has investigated how effective students learn on their own. He has discovered remarkable similarity in the techniques that successful students use to read, study, write, and prepare for examinations, regardless of whether they attend schools in the inner city or the suburbs, in the Northeast or Southwest, and in the United States or as far away as Australia. He teaches graduate-level courses on self-regulated learning processes at the City University of New York. Sebastian Bonner is a doctoral student who has taught undergraduate courses in self-regulation to classes of future teachers and has conducted impressive case studies of individualized tutoring of students experiencing academic difficulty. Robert Kovach is a high-school social studies teacher who has developed innovative procedures for assessing his students' self-regulated methods of learning and their understanding of the effectiveness of those methods. We decided to write this guide to share our collective insights because each of us has profited personally from the use of these processes and has seen their power with our students. The impact of these processes extended beyond students' academic achievement. We have witnessed their self-efficacy beliefs grow as they became more self-regulatory—until they, like the Confucian fisherman, could personally feed their hunger for knowledge for a lifetime.

ACKNOWLEDGEMENTS

We would like to acknowledge the assistance on earlier drafts of this teacher's guide of the following students, teachers and educational psychologists: Alexandra M. Arlak, student at Leonia Middle School, Leonia, NJ; Jed Wang Bonner, student at Manhattan Country School in New York City; Maryann Dragunas, Paul D. Schreiber High School (SHS), Port Washington, NY; Shirley Feldmann, professor of educational psychology at the Graduate School and University Center, City University of New York (CUNY); Bert Flugman, director of the Center of Advanced Study in Education, CUNY; Martin Hamburger, SHS; Manuel Martinez-Pons, professor of education, Brooklyn College, CUNY; Barbara L. McCombs, series editor at Mid-Continental Regional Educational Laboratory; Ann Mingorance, SHS; Sharon L. McNeely, series editor at Northeastern Illinois University; Anne Simmons, art teacher at Hart Magnet Elementary School in Stanford, CT; and Ellen Zimmerman, SHS. We are grateful for their thoughtful suggestions and creative insights.

introduction

In this age of information, the explosion of knowledge and the need for technical skill has posed tremendous new burdens on our schools, families, employers, and communities. The traditional view of education as an activity for the young is being increasingly supplanted by contemporary demands for lifelong learning. But how well have we equipped our youth to assume the burden of learning for themselves?

According to most indicators, there is reason to be concerned. Our students' completion of homework remains low, their dropout rate from schools is more than 40% in many urban areas, and their literacy rate is a major source of social concern. Employers are unable to hire significant numbers of young Americans because they lack requisite reading, writing, and computational skills. These problems have led to numerous efforts to reform or reinvigorate the educational system—often in the form of new goals for our schools and teachers to accomplish (e.g., *America 2000: An Education Strategy*, 1990). The attainment of educational goals, such as improved academic attendance, test scores, and motivation, however, is not exclusively under the control of teachers and schools. In fact, educators are just one force in a complex learning process that involves many others, including peers, parents, the media, and especially the students themselves.

> Academic self-regulation refers to self-generated thoughts, feelings, and actions intended to attain specific educational goals, such as analyzing a reading assignment, preparing to take a test, or writing a paper.

SELF-REGULATION AND LEARNING

In contrast to this teacher-control assumption, researchers have revealed the essential role of specific self-regulatory activities that achieving students use to learn (see Pintrich & De Groot, 1990; Pressley & Woloshyn, 1995; Schunk & Zimmerman, 1994; Zimmerman & Schunk, 1989). Compared with low-achieving students, high achievers report setting more specific learning goals for themselves, using more strategies to learn, self-monitoring learning progress more frequently, and more systematically adapting their efforts on the basis of learning outcomes. Self-monitoring is the deliberate observation of covert and overt aspects of one's performance outcomes on a given task, such as comprehending while reading. High achievers feel self-efficacious and personally responsible for their control of the academic-learning process. Self-efficacy refers to self-perceptions or beliefs of capability to learn or perform tasks at designated levels (Bandura, 1986), such as getting a B on a test.

This book provides an instructional model for teaching essential study skills to middle- and high-school students during homework and studying. The examples are drawn from the middle-school years because this is the age period when most students begin to experience significant homework and studying responsibilities and when failures to self-manage these activities can erode their academic identities. Although components of self-regulation, such as cognitive-strategy acquisition, should be taught from the early elementary school years, we believe the metacognitive benefits of comprehensive self-regulatory training will become especially evident during the middle-school years and thereafter (Zimmerman & Martinez-Pons, 1990). The book is organized to help teachers implement a *self-regulatory cycle* (for a glossary of italicized terms, please refer to page 139) that assists students to self-observe and self-evaluate their effectiveness, set goals and use learning strategies, self-monitor changes, and adjust their strategic methods. Importantly, the self-regulatory cycle gives students a sense of personal control that has been shown to be a major source of intrinsic motivation to continue learning on one's own (Zimmerman, 1985, 1995). We will provide specific tools to convert your classroom into self-regulated learning academies, wherein students give as much attention to their methods of learning as they do to the outcomes. Such classrooms are designed to draw on peer modeling and feedback as well as teacher resources in the process of becoming self-regulatory.

> A self-regulatory cycle is designed to enhance not only students' learning but also their perception of self-efficacy or control over the learning process.

RATIONALE AND GOALS

In the following sections of this guide, we will illustrate how a self-regulatory learning cycle can be implemented to enable middle- and high-school students to develop five essential academic skills: (a) planning and using study time more effectively, (b) understanding and summarizing text material better, (c) improving methods of note taking, (d) anticipating and preparing better for examinations, and (e) writing more effectively. Although this book is written for teachers, its purpose is to empower students to self-observe their current study practices more accurately, to ascertain for themselves which study methods are ineffective and replace them with better ones, and to be more personally aware of their improved effectiveness—that is, we want to show them how to become smart learners! We will discuss how you can organize classroom and homework activities to achieve these self-regulatory ends and how you can shift your role to that of a self-regulatory coach or consultant. In addition to providing monitoring forms for each area of learning and checklists for implementing self-regulatory training over 5-week modules, we will illustrate exemplary interventions with specific case studies of students like those in your class. Finally, we will discuss the instructional capabilities that you will need to implement a self- regulatory approach to student learning.

goal 1

Understanding the Principles of
Self-Regulated Learning

This chapter introduces two typical students who are experiencing self-regulated learning deficiencies, and it describes how you can help them and similar students by converting your classroom into an academy for teaching self-regulatory processes. These students will be revisited during subsequent chapters in this guidebook as they try to master key skills underlying proficient learning, such as academic time planning and management, text comprehension and summarization, and test anticipation and preparation. Self-regulated learning academies are designed to teach these skills on the basis of a cyclic model of self-regulatory training. We will discuss your role in implementing this cycle of self-regulation and some of the rewards your students and you will enjoy when they acquire a self-regulatory level of academic proficiency.

STUDENTS WITH SELF-REGULATED LEARNING DEFICIENCIES

Research suggests that most teachers are aware of their students who have self-regulatory problems (Zimmerman & Martinez-Pons, 1988). However, the exact nature of the deficiencies is often unclear. We will illustrate our application of self-regulated learning techniques with two typical students who are experiencing problems.

> *Calvin*, a bright sixth grader who has never experienced much success in school, has dreamed of achieving better and even thinks he may try to be the first person in his family to graduate from high school. Considering his family's low level of education, it is not surprising that Calvin has not developed many essential study skills and has many unfortunate habits, such as procrastinating, skimming reading assignments, cramming for tests at the last minute, and writing in a haphazard manner. He has a low sense of self-efficacy about improving his grades in school and generally appears poorly motivated in class.
>
> *Maria* is an eighth-grade student who enjoys a wide social network. She diligently completes her work but only in a

superficial way. Although she tries hard in school, school work is less important to her than her friends, and as a result, she gets only average grades. She is very popular among her classmates, and she usually "studies" daily with friends—sharing answers to math or science problems and reading her assignments cursorily between extended discussions about the day's events. Maria prepares minimally for tests, usually cramming the night before the exam, and her writing skills are a year below grade level. She has only a moderate amount of self-efficacy about doing well academically and tries not to think much about the future.

We will revisit Calvin and Maria throughout this book to find out (a) how they use essential study skills, (b) whether they can learn to self-regulate those skills to a greater degree, and (c) whether self-regulated learning experiences will improve their sense of self-efficacy regarding their academic future.

SELF-REGULATED LEARNING: THE ACADEMY MODEL

Self-regulatory models of instruction focus on students' use of specific processes to motivate and guide their learning. Although teachers seldom give self-regulatory training in traditional classrooms, tutors or coaches of individuals or small groups of students use it more widely. Research on the development of expert skills in performance arts, sports, chess, and writing shows that students' methods of learning and practice are far more important than their personal talent.

Ericsson and Charness (1994) noted a number of common social-learning and self-regulatory features in the case histories of elite performers. From early ages, these future experts were tutored strategically by master teachers (often a parent). The child's eventual level of expertise depended more on consistent goal-directed practice than anything else. Parents were helped to arrange their child's life to ensure learning by eliminating competing demands and by spacing practice to reduce fatigue. Their coaches and tutors not only stressed deliberate goal-directed practice but also encouraged their parents to monitor and reinforce their youngster for small improvements in skill. Making practice a regular part of the child's daily activities was designed to ensure that the skill became automatic. Interestingly, research on the development of high levels of performance indicates that precocious children show the identical sequence of stages seen in typical youngsters; they differ only in the speed of acquisition.

Notice the key role that parents play in valuing and supporting their children's development of skill. The capability to self-regulate emerges naturally in a social climate of dedication and common purpose, such as in a family or an effective school (Schunk & Zimmerman, 1996).

We suggest that an instructional model involving explicit training in goal setting, strategy use, self-monitoring, and systematic practice can be used in classroom situations. These self-disciplinary processes underlying expert mastery are given greater emphasis in schools organized as *learning academies* around disciplines such as music, dance, art, military regimen, or science, and as a result, the curriculum focuses on developing improved methods of performance as well as imparting established knowledge. We believe that key aspects of this educational model can be introduced by teachers during homework activities. Unlike traditional high schools, academies are designed to advance a discipline as well as to provide instruction to the next generation.

This behavioral focus of academies influences the form of learning, with greater emphasis placed on expert and peer modeling, direct social feedback for performance efforts, and practice routines involving specific goals and methods of self-monitoring. For example, dance academies place hand rails next to mirrors to make it easier for students to self-observe their stylistic form as they practice ballet movements, such as pirouettes. The distinction between pupil and teacher is less pronounced in academies, and greater reliance is placed on tutoring and coaching during actual performance efforts rather than on lecturing in passive classroom settings.

Of course, parents often choose to enroll their children in an academy because of its reputation and relevance to the youngsters' future, and this belief undoubtedly plays an important role in youngsters' initial commitment to learn. However, if the process of learning does not become self-sustaining for the students, their motivation would soon flag (as it sometimes does). We have evidence that academic self-motivation grows initially from parental goal expectations but ultimately from acquired academic standards, perceived self-efficacy, and personal goal setting (Zimmerman, Bandura, & Martinez-Pons, 1992).

The teacher in an academy plays a key role in socially conveying the value of becoming academically self-regulative and the commitment that is needed to achieve it. We have found that even skeptical, streetwise students can be induced to give these processes a fair test if the potential advantages of becoming a smart learner are described, namely, being *a controller* of the learning process rather than a victim of it. They can acquire the savvy and

> Academies provide a performance context where standards, personal goals, and a sense of self-efficacy are mutually valued and can emerge as students watch expert models' and peers' self-directed practice.

personal resources to overcome obstacles, such as poor learning environments, rambling lectures, poorly written books, and difficult tests. Smart learners ultimately learn more with less effort once they discover the processes that work best for them, and this is where self-monitoring and other self-regulatory processes come into play.

By making students' learning methods and techniques a primary focus of homework and by helping them to monitor and interpret their outcomes strategically, teachers can convert their classrooms into learning academies. The ultimate psychological advantages of this shift in academic focus to *learning methods* are profound because one's progress in mastering methods of learning precedes improved learning outcomes (Bandura, 1986; Schunk & Swartz, 1993; Zimmerman & Bandura, 1994). When students' perceive a teacher's primary goal as conveying how to learn, they will relax their self-defenses and will seek assistance more readily, often in the form of modeling and coaching from teachers and knowledgeable peers (Schunk & Zimmerman, 1996). Before we discuss how learning academies can be organized as part of regular classroom, we should consider the cyclic properties of a self-regulated approach to learning.

Learning *strategies* can be taught successfully from the elementary-school to the collegiate level as long as they are integrated within a larger framework of self-regulatory training (Pressley & Woloshyn, 1995; Zimmerman, 1989). Despite their potential power, strategies are not a panacea for learning difficulties because their effectiveness depends on various personal and contextual factors. Many students who have knowledge of a learning strategy will not continue to use it unless their knowledge leads to appropriate goal setting, accurate strategic process and outcome self-monitoring, and greater self-efficacy.

> When self-regulatory processes play an integral role in the development and use of study skills, students become more acutely aware of improvements in their academic achievement and experience a heightened sense of personal efficacy.

To acquire mastery of optimal studying techniques, students need to make multiple efforts to reveal the strategic components that are responsible for successes as well as those in need of further improvement. No single strategy will work for all students, and few strategies can be implemented fully during the first effort. A strategy becomes powerful when its implementation is self-monitored and its outcomes are self-evaluated favorably. Homework can be structured to enhance students' use of powerful learning strategies and their self-monitoring of goal attainment. When students are given no explicit training in homework and studying strategies, they are often unable to devise techniques personally to improve their success or self-monitoring, and their self-evaluations inevitably suffer (Zimmerman, & Martinez-Pons, 1986, 1988, 1990). For example, students tend to underestimate the difficulty of tests and overestimate their preparation, and this leads to poor test performance (Ghatala, Levin, Foorman, & Pressley, 1989).

Historically, teachers have used homework as a major source of academic skill practice, and we propose to expand homework exercises to include self-regulatory training as well as content mastery. In this way, typical classrooms can be converted into academies for advanced methods for studying incorporating a self-regulatory learning cycle. This cycle, depicted in Figure 1, involves four interrelated processes that are defined below.

☐ *Self-evaluation and monitoring* occur when students judge their personal effectiveness, often from observations and recordings of prior performances and outcomes.

☐ *Goal setting and strategic planning* occur when students analyze the learning task, set specific learning goals, and plan or refine the strategy to attain the goal.

☐ *Strategy-implementation monitoring* occurs when students try to execute a strategy in structured contexts and to monitor their accuracy in implementing it.

☐ *Strategic-outcome monitoring* occurs when students focus their attention on links between learning outcomes and strategic processes to determine effectiveness.

Figure 1 *A cyclic model of self-regulated learning.*

The first step in the cycle involves evaluating one's current level of learning on a task. As students begin to study an unfamiliar topic, they have only a vague sense of the effectiveness of their approach. Keeping performance records can greatly improve the accuracy of a learner's self-evaluations. For example, often students are unaware of how much study time they waste until they keep a detailed log. Self-tests or feedback from their teacher, peers, or parents can assist self-evaluation.

> By establishing this self-regulatory cycle, teachers help students learn to recognize and appreciate links between their study behaviors and learning outcomes.

The second step in the cycle involves analyzing the learning task, setting goals, and planning or refining a learning strategy. As students begin to learn an unfamiliar topic, they have little ability to break the task into components and often fail to set specific goals for themselves or develop an effective learning strategy. Teachers can instruct students how to analyze tasks, set effective goals, and choose the right strategy. For example, students who procrastinate about writing a term paper can observe their teacher demonstrate how to create an outline for a similar topic, to schedule writing sessions for various subheadings, and to edit the final copy.

The third step involves implementing the learner's strategy choice, which depends on previously used strategies, feedback from peers or teachers, and self-monitoring. As students begin to implement a new strategy, they often lapse into more familiar methods unless they monitor their strategic performance closely, such as by keeping records of strategy steps they used. With continued practice, especially in structured settings where feedback is unambiguous, they learn to execute the strategy eventually without specific attention.

The fourth step involves expanding the learner's monitoring to include performance outcomes associated with strategic variations to determine effectiveness. For example, a student who uses a grouping strategy to memorize key concepts in geography will learn that meaningful categories, such as lakes, deserts, and mountains, will work better than arbitrary categories, such as words that begin with the letter l, d or m. The effectiveness of any learning strategy depends on a number of task, contextual, and personal factors—which can fluctuate.

A memory strategy that works for a multiple-choice test may be poor for a completion test or may not work well on certain topics. The point is that self-regulated learners must constantly self-monitor learning outcomes and vary their strategic approach to compensate for intervening events, such as variations in the type of test questions that are encountered (Butler & Winne, 1995; Zimmerman & Paulsen, 1995).

As students begin to monitor the effectiveness of a newly acquired strategy, they are often unsure about which parts of the strategy are responsible for which outcome features. However, with careful self-monitoring during practice, they eventually acquire knowledge of these differential effects. Self-monitoring of strategic outcomes is essential for self-regulation because it produces corrective cognitive, emotional, and behavioral *reactive effects*, such as strategy improvements following unfavorable results. In contrast, students who are unprepared for negative learning outcomes often perceive them as "failures" and react unproductively, sometimes giving up because of feelings of anxiety or helplessness.

Self-monitoring of one's current level of skill may indicate that the initial goals are too ambitious or that a particular strategy needs adjustment because it is not paying off. For example, a student trying to memorize all new vocabulary words in a chapter in Spanish using an inefficient rehearsal strategy might decide (after monitoring the poor results) to try an elaboration strategy or to focus on only key words in the chapter. Adverse results can also lead self-regulated students to seek additional social guidance from a teacher or knowledgeable peer.

> The model is cyclic because self-monitoring on each learning trial provides information that can change subsequent goals, strategies, or performance efforts.

Self-regulation is not an isolated endeavor but involves the self-directed use of social assistance and the use of informational resources (Newman, 1994). Although some common learning strategies will be mentioned for illustrative purposes in the following chapters, we will emphasize instead the need to be strategic. To learn an academic skill efficiently, students should focus primarily on deficient components and should modify or develop a strategy that is suitable for mastering them by following the four cyclic steps.

Let's turn next to the issue of applying these four steps to learning in a regular class.

APPLYING SELF-REGULATORY PROCESSES IN THE CLASSROOM

Consider the example of a seventh-grade girl who is doing poorly in a history course. According to the first step in Figure 2, she needs to self-evaluate her studying and test-preparation processes by keeping a detailed record of them. From this self-recorded information, the teacher can help her trace her poor test performance to poor comprehension of difficult reading material.

Once the general deficiency area is identified, the teacher begins step two and assists the girl in breaking the reading-comprehension task into components, such as locating main ideas, and in setting specific component goals

> Asking students to rate their self-efficacy after studying increases self-monitoring during the study session and awareness of which goals were actually accomplished.

for herself with regard to a series of paragraphs from the book. The student must decide also on a strategy to improve each form of reading comprehension. For example, to help identify main ideas, the teacher may suggest focusing initially on the first sentence of each paragraph and then scanning the others to see whether any other sentence better captures the meaning of that paragraph. If not, the first sentence is chosen. The selected sentences could be emphasized using a highlighting pen or by recording in a separate list. She may need to watch the teacher or a peer demonstrate this sentence-selection strategy to make it more concrete and hear its conditions of effectiveness described.

The third step in the self-regulation cycle involves implementing the strategy. At the outset, the girl may need social feedback from her teacher or a competent classmate who is good at the skill concerning her accuracy in iden-

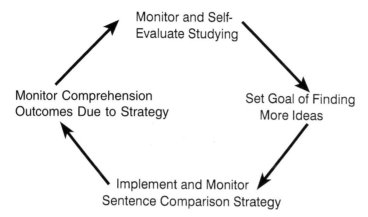

Figure 2 *Self-regulated learning of reading-comprehension skills.*

tifying main ideas. This will help her to self-monitor more effectively on her own.

Once she masters the sentence-selection strategy, she will begin step four and broaden the scope of her self-monitoring to include reading-comprehension outcomes as well as strategic processes. Teachers can facilitate this shift in self-monitoring by asking for frequent comprehension self-efficacy ratings and by giving short history tests to provide external feedback. When classroom test results are compared with these self-efficacy ratings, students' inaccuracies in self-judgment become obvious and can lead to more realistic self-monitoring during future study sessions.

The girl's self-evaluations of monitored strategic outcomes may reveal that her strategy of finding the main ideas is only partially effective in improving comprehension and does not work with paragraphs that lack a topic sentence. The teacher may need to suggest further strategic refinement by including other strategies to aid comprehension, such as self-questioning or summarizing. Each of these types of strategies can be acquired by cycling through each of the steps again. After these other comprehension strategies are mastered and integrated with the main idea strategy, the student will be able to shift strategies flexibly depending on her comprehension monitoring and the type of written material that she encounters. Thus, implementation of comprehension learning strategies adheres directly to the cyclic model of self-regulation described earlier.

The Teacher's Role in Developing Self-Regulated Students

As we alluded to earlier, the role of teachers in developing self-regulated students is different from traditional classes where the instructor emphasizes subject content goals, monitors students' progress, and modulates the pace of learning for the entire class. In classes based on a learning-academy model, the teacher shifts the responsibility to students by (a) asking them to self-monitor, (b) assisting them to analyze their own data either individually or in small groups, and (c) helping them set goals and choose strategies in light of self-monitored outcomes. Second, the teacher may teach self-regulatory techniques by modeling self-monitoring and strategy-selection procedures, such as (a) demonstrating his or her own use of process-monitoring forms, (b) hypothesizing strategy choices and evaluating outcomes, and (c) refining strategies in light of the results gained. Third, and perhaps most important, the teacher encourages students to self-monitor so they may refine their self-regulatory strategies. A teacher's support when students' strategies do not seem to work can be pivotal to their continuation of a self-regulatory approach.

In this way, teachers seeking to develop self-regulated students shift the responsibility for the learning process to the students. Like the faculty of a special academy, they focus on teaching students to use specific standards to self-monitor, to set appropriate learning goals for themselves, to adopt strategies to achieve these goals, and to acquire a sense of self-efficacy about eventually attaining mastery. These teachers concentrate first on students' learning methods before they attend to learning outcomes. They function more like tutors or coaches by providing specific, personalized feedback instead of merely presenting general information to students. Their goal is to transform their classes into academies where students can become smart learners.

> Teachers can shift responsibility for the learning process by helping their students develop self-regulatory skill.

Five Skills for Proficient Academic Learning

How often have you heard students express the following frustrations: "I can't get my homework done on time, and I always have to cram for tests." These comments reflect a deficiency in their time planning and management skills. Complaints such as, "I don't spend time on homework because I would have to restudy the material before tests anyway" and "I can't take good notes during class" are examples of problems in *text summarization* and *note taking*. "I never know if I'll do well on tests" indicates problems with *test preparation*, and "I hate essay questions" bespeaks poor *writing* skills.

Teachers hear these cries for help and often respond with admonitions, such as try harder, start studying earlier, pay more attention, wake up earlier, get your priorities straight, take better notes, or ask one of the other students. These tips, which are typical efforts to instill greater self-regulation in students, are seldom effective unless they are implemented according to a systematic instructional approach. By applying cyclic self-regulatory methods to improving basic study skills, students will grow in their capability and confidence to use the skills on their own.

Teachers should consider the value of self-regulatory training with these five studying skills because of widespread evidence that they are not generally well-developed or used efficiently by students (DeWitt, 1992; Kozol, 1985). Each skill is essential for proficient academic learning. Additional benefits can be gained by acquiring all five skills because they are mutually reinforcing—that is, gains in one skill are conducive to gains in the others. Each of these skills relates to the academic work that students do during private study—the context in which most self-regulated learning takes place.

The key to the development of these skills is the systematic application of self-regulatory methods, which students can learn to apply as part of their daily class assignments. The teacher's primary role in promoting self-regulated learning is to help students assume responsibility for their own learning progress. "Developing self-regulated learners" refers to students' growth toward proficiency in self-regulatory processes that underlie their learning, such as self-monitoring, setting goals, and adapting learning strategies. In this regard, our emphasis is mainly on what students do, perhaps with some teacher assistance at the outset but eventually on their own, to manage and feel self-efficacious about their learning.

> The teachers' goal is to work themselves out of the job of managing their students' learning.

Recent research on self-regulatory processes has made this task much easier, and the implications of that research is the topic of this book. Our aim is for teachers to help their students understand and achieve the empowerment that comes from self-regulated learning.

Inaugurating the Cycle of Self-Regulation

In succeeding chapters, we will demonstrate how a cyclic self-regulatory approach to learning can be used to teach these five essential study skills sequentially. Teachers may choose to implement this approach with all five skills or with fewer than the five that are described. The selected learning skills are not meant to be exhaustive but rather are designed to illustrate how a self-regulatory approach can be used with different types of students. For additional strategies in each skill area, readers are referred to *Suggested Readings* at the end of the goal unit. The choice of which learning skills to implement should be based on the interests and needs of the students. The self-regulative approach we offer can be applied to developing whatever skills the teacher wishes to emphasize.

The self-regulative cycle can be implemented in the following way.

Self-Evaluation and Monitoring

☐ The teacher distributes forms for students to monitor specific aspects of their studying. Examples of these forms appear throughout this book. Monitoring is designed to complement required academic exercises such as reading assignments, note taking, and test preparation.

□ The teacher presents students with daily assignments to develop their skills and a weekly quiz for them to assess the effectiveness of their familiar methods. We have found that assignment and quiz dates should be announced in advance so that systematic preparation is rewarded.

□ During each class for a week, the teacher shifts the focus from merely assessing the accuracy of students' homework to identifying their processes of studying by having them exchange work with their peers. After a class discussion of optimal learning strategies and outcomes, the peers will evaluate the homework and self-monitoring forms and make suggestions how the students can improve their methods of studying. Finally, teachers will then collect the homework for grading purposes and review the peers' suggestions.

Planning and Goal Setting

□ After a week of monitoring and after the first graded exercise, the teacher solicits students' perceptions of strengths and weaknesses of their approaches to their studying methods. The teacher emphasizes the link between learning methods and learning outcomes and encourages students to pursue a high level of specificity in their evaluations.

□ The teacher and peers suggest specific strategies that students might use to improve their learning methods. Students may adapt the teacher's recommendations or devise their own. They aim to improve their achievement through a specific set of goals.

Strategy Implementation and Monitoring

□ The students monitor the extent to which they actually implement the new strategies. Some students rapidly gain familiarity with their new strategic efforts; they vicariously learn from their peer's variations on the same efforts. Other students have difficulty adjusting to new procedures. Different students take different lengths of time to change their habits.

☐ The teacher's role is to ensure that these new learning methods are publicly discussed.

☐ The teacher continues to provide graded opportunities for students to gauge the implementation of their new strategies.

Outcome Monitoring and Strategy Refinement

☐ Once the students have assimilated the new strategy, they should begin to monitor their personal effectiveness in using the strategies. The teacher encourages them to optimize their academic outcomes by varying their learning strategies and determining the most effective combination.

☐ The teacher continues to provide graded opportunities for students to gauge the effectiveness of their new strategies and refine their use.

☐ The teacher helps students summarize their cyclic strategic efforts by reviewing each step of the self-regulatory process—the progress they made, the hurdles they overcame, and the gains in grades and self-confidence they achieved.

In addition to their overall role in guiding class implementation of a cyclic self-regulatory approach, teachers can provide four types of individual support to students:

☐ *Modeling*: They can demonstrate personally how to self-regulate processes that students find difficult, such as strategic thinking patterns, problem-solving approaches, and accurate self-evaluations.

☐ *Encouragement*: As students attempt to imitate the teacher, their first efforts usually are rough approximations. Rather than criticize students' failure to display immediate proficiency, teachers can emphasize the students' successes and encourage further attempts to improve.

☐ *Task and strategic analysis*: Teachers can provide specific assistance to help students break academic tasks down into components and develop a new learning strategy for them. It is not assumed that students possess the necessary analytic skills to identify their specific study problems. Teachers may need to help students to set appropriate goals and choose effective strategies at the outset.

☐ *Outcome checking and strategy refinement*: As students shift their attention from strategy imitation to learning-outcome optimization, many of them need suggestions about how to evaluate academic outcomes accurately and which aspects of their strategy are most helpful or need to be altered. Teachers can check their students' grading of one another's homework to ensure accuracy and can provide recommendations regarding how the strategy can be modified to make it more productive. Some students will be lax in their grading, and this can not only mislead their peers but can also undermine subsequent self-evaluations of their own work.

ON THE ROAD TO REWARDS

Teachers who convert their classroom into academies for self-regulated learning convey the message that each student bears the ultimate responsibility for becoming educated and that they are available to help these youth succeed on their personal journey. Another message is that learning is a personal experience that requires active, informed, and dedicated participation by the student.

Like students entering a music academy, self-regulated learners must initially evaluate their entering study skills, set an appropriate goal for themselves, imitate experts' strategies for attaining their goals, and self-monitor their daily practice efforts carefully—buoyed by small improvements and determined to eliminate unproductive habits. This academy educational model can be implemented through a cycle of self-regulation during regular class assignments, which cover approximately 5 weeks for each of the following study skills: (a) time planning and management, (b) text comprehension and summarization, (c) classroom note taking, (d) test anticipation and preparation, and (e) writing. Each study skill will be introduced subsequently as separate instructional goals in this manual. If the training for each study skill is implemented sequentially, the entire program will require 25 to 30 weeks. Although expanding homework assignments to include self-regulatory processes does require additional time for both students and teachers, it will contribute substantially to the effectiveness of the curriculum.

> Learning is not something that can be done *for* students, rather it is something that is done *by* them.

1 Which students in your class might have significant self-regulated learning deficiencies?

2 Which aspects of an academy model of self-regulated learning do you presently use in your classroom, and which ones would you need to add if you decide to adopt the model?

3 Describe which of the five skills for proficient academic learning you would select first to help students in your class and how it could help them improve their academic achievement.

SUGGESTED READINGS

Snyder, B., & Pressley, M. (1995). Introduction to cognitive strategy instruction. In M. Pressley, V. Woloshyn, J. Burkell, T. Cariglia-Bull, L. Lysynchuk, J. A. McGoldrick, B. Schneider, B.L. Snyder, & S. Symons (Eds.), *Cognitive strategy instruction that really improves children's academic performance* (2nd ed., pp. 1–18). Cambridge, MA: Brookline Books.

Weinstein, C. E. (1992). Working hard is not the same as working smart. *Innovation Abstract, 14*(5), 1–2.

Zimmerman, B. J., & Risemberg, R. (in press). Self-regulatory dimensions of academic learning and motivation. In G. D. Phye (Ed.), *Handbook of academic learning: the construction of knowledge*. San Diego, CA: Academic Press.

goal 2

Developing Time Planning
and Management Skills

The effective use of one's study time is essential to academic success because insufficient time compels expediency—the very antithesis of self-regulated learning. To enhance students' regulation of study time, a teacher can first, in a narrower sense, orchestrate events to help students understand that time is a crucial learning resource and that efficient time management can bolster learning and perceptions of self-efficacy, whereas inefficient time use can depress them. Second, in a broader sense, a teacher aims to help students induce from their learning experience which things they are doing efficiently.

SELF-EVALUATION AND MONITORING

Students need to record specific features of their study hours to be able to evaluate their time use accurately. To establish a context within which students can evaluate their time planning and management activities, the teacher prepares a series of several weeks worth of reading assignments with accompanying questions and weekly quizzes on the content of these assignments. The reading assignments, questions, and quizzes should be roughly equivalent in scope, length, and difficulty. These are important requirements because students need consistent academic challenges if they are to self-evaluate the effects of their strategic efforts accurately over time.

Educators have long recommended that students be assigned questions at the completion of reading assignments and that they be regularly quizzed on the material they have learned. Our requirements for this self-regulatory exercise in time planning and management are consonant with such recommendations. Following each homework assignment, teachers may present their classes with evaluative criteria for the answers and ask students to exchange their answers and provide feedback regarding one another's work. Similar peer feedback routines can be followed immediately after quizzes. Peer evaluations can have an important advantage: When teachers collect the homework or quiz results to grade a student, they will be able to gauge the peer's understanding of the judgmental criteria as well as the student's strategic skill. Evaluative accuracy is an essential component of self-regulation.

Assigning readings, providing questions, and adminis-

> By promoting students' awareness of their use of study time, a teacher sets the stage for them to assume a greater role in regulating other aspects of their learning.

tering the regular quizzes are sound instructional practices, but in and of themselves, they do not ensure self-regulation. The additional element to conventional instructional practices is student self-monitoring, which can be invoked, for example, by asking students to keep consistent records of how they spend their time during conventional assignments. Monitoring should be kept simple. The few elements we have included on the chart below (see Exhibit 1) would provide students with a detailed look at the activities associated with their regular completion of typical homework assignments. Teachers should feel free to adapt the time-monitoring chart to their classes' needs or to individual students who might be experiencing unusual time use difficulties.

Self-efficacy is an important variable for students to monitor because it focuses attention on their beliefs about the effectiveness of their learning methods.

Teachers should provide students with an objective way to monitor their self-efficacy for attaining their learning outcomes (i.e., quiz grades or homework scores). Although there are a number of ways to assess self-efficacy, we recommend one method that is easy to compute in which students rate their self-efficacy at being able to achieve an expected score on the upcoming quiz. We will illustrate this method with the following example.

Let us assume that the weekly quizzes consist of 10 questions, with every correct answer receiving a point. The teacher asks the students to estimate the score they expect to receive on the quiz and then to rate their confidence about attaining at least that score using a 3-point scale (representing *not very sure, quite sure,* and *absolutely sure*). To adjust the estimated score for differences in confidence, the following weighting procedure should be used. For the rating of not very sure, a point is subtracted from the estimated score (-1); for the rating of quite sure, no points are added or subtracted from the estimated score (0); for the rating of absolutely sure, a point is added to the estimated score ($+1$).

Self-efficacy is defined as the estimated score after the point adjustment. For example, a girl who expects to get a score of 6 but is not very sure (-1) about receiving at

EXHIBIT 1	Study Time Self-Monitoring Form						

Date	Assignment	Time Started	Time Spent	Study Context			Self-Efficacy
				Where?	With Whom?	Distractions?	

least that score, would have a self-efficacy total of 5 (i.e., $6 - 1 = 5$). She actually took the test and received a 7 on it. The next week, she might estimate a 7 for the quiz and rate her self-efficacy as quite sure (0). Her self-efficacy would then increase to 7 (i.e., $7 + 0 = 7$). She received an 8 on this test, surpassing her expectations, so she then estimated a score of 8 for a third quiz with a self-efficacy level of quite sure. Her score on the third quiz was 8 as she expected. To interpret these changes in self-efficacy most effectively, the girl should graph her estimated quiz score on a scale of 1 to 10 and indicate her self-efficacy. This graphing will allow the expected grades to be plotted on the same graph as the girl's test results (see Figure 3). Students who misjudge their self-efficacy will quickly see these errors and will adjust their standards when judging their self-efficacy in the future. The goal of self-efficacy monitoring is to make students more accurate in predicting their learning; however, being slightly optimistic can assist motivation without detracting from learning. —

> Self-efficacy ratings not only are informative to students but also produce self-regulatory reactions, such as changing their self-evaluative standards or increasing studying to score better on weekly quizzes.

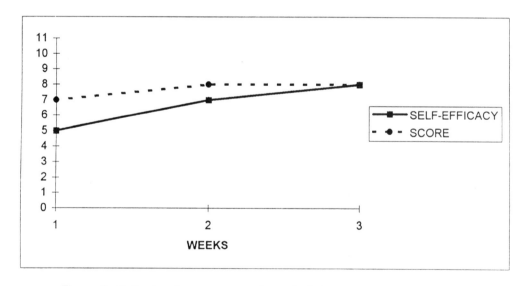

Figure 3 *Girl's plotted outcome scores by week of time management intervention.*

This same self-efficacy rating procedure should be used by students on a daily basis to self-evaluate their studying. For example, after reading a chapter in biology one evening, the girl might estimate being quite sure she would receive at least an 8 if the teacher gave her a 10- question quiz on the material she had just read. By rating and graphing self-efficacy for each episode of studying, she will begin to self-evaluate changes in her effectiveness and to use these ratings to prepare for weekly quizzes based on multiple homework assignments. Self-efficacy ratings also can be helpful to teachers because they reveal students who are unduly pessimistic or overly optimistic about their studying or test preparation. Pessimism can lead to poor motivation, and over-optimism can lead to insufficient preparation.

During the first week of the exercise, students will gain a detailed view of how they manage their study time, how well they fulfill their homework requirements, and how much learning they achieve. The self-monitoring form will help students discern and respond to the relation between their time management practices and their learning achievement. During the first week of this exercise, it is more important that students establish consistent self-monitoring habits than that they form accurate conclusions about their time management skills.

To understand how time planning and management comes under self-regulatory control, let us turn back to Calvin and Maria and their differing uses of study time. We will begin by examining the outcomes of their initial self-monitoring.

> *Calvin* has a habit of starting his arithmetic homework late in the evening while watching television. As usual, Calvin began his homework at 9:00 each night. He stopped when the half-hour sitcom ended, regardless of whether he had completed his assignment. Just before class, he spent 5 minutes "guesstimating" answers to some of the remaining problems. He averaged only 2 out of 10 on his homework assignments,

and his self-efficacy for these assignments has been low at 3. For his weekly arithmetic quiz, he rated his self-efficacy at 4, indicating he was not very sure of getting even a five (i.e., $5 - 1 = 4$) on it, and he earned only a 4 on that quiz.

Maria generally does her math problems with a friend each day, and during her recording period, she spent 45 minutes each afternoon "working" with her best friend in the cafeteria. Although some of her time was consumed in discussions about boyfriends, she and her friend did manage to get through the problems. Together, they worked out the answers to the assigned problems. Maria was quite sure about their answers to the homework problems, but she did not feel very sure about being tested on the material. She rated her self-efficacy on the mathematics homework at 6, indicating she was not very sure of getting a 7 ($7 - 1 = 6$). Her homework scores for the week averaged 7, and she scored a 7 on the quiz.

GOAL SETTING AND STRATEGIC PLANNING

The teacher initiates the next phase of self-regulatory–skill development at the beginning of the second week by devoting one half of the class period to guide students in evaluating their time-management processes and setting process goals for developing their skills. Teachers can use this exercise to help students analyze their process records. The teacher can demonstrate quantitative analyses, such as creating a simple line graph. For example, students plot three lines: one line for time spent, one line for their self-efficacy ratings, and a third line for their homework scores. These three lines run horizontally across a grid representing the days of the week. Students can try to link variations in these three measures with the records they maintained of their study context. It may be helpful for students to evaluate their process records in small groups, where they can compare their effectiveness with their peers' methods of managing time.

When students understand their individual patterns of time use, the teacher can encourage them to develop strategies for changing the way they plan and manage their study schedules.

The teacher can show how students, such as Calvin and Maria might choose or develop time-management strategies. The instructor can model how to use an analytical framework in which students think about three dimensions of study—regularity, context, and quality. *Regularity* refers to the amount and consistency of studying, which can be inferred from the date and time columns of Exhibit 1. *Context* refers to where and with whom one studies and to the presence of distractions, which can be deduced from study context columns of Exhibit 1. Finally, the quality of one's studying can be judged from the self-efficacy ratings in Exhibit 1.

For example, a student's time records may show that studying before dinner in the evening by himself may lead to higher quality homework than after dinner or with a study partner. The teacher can follow this type of analytic modeling with peer group or whole class discussion of these dimensions. Often peers can get involved with one another's strategic adjustments to time management in far greater detail than can the teacher. They can offer one another suggestions for resolving difficulties and, in some cases, can even serve as models.

Selected Time Planning and Management Strategies

Below are listed some commonly used strategies to plan and manage one's time. This list is not meant to be exhaustive but merely illustrative of strategies that have been effective. Students may wish to refer to other sources (e.g., Ellis, 1994) or to develop their own strategies. No strategy is universally effective, but each strategy has specific effects and works well with certain students in specific contexts. Therefore, each strategy should be chosen only when it is appropriate, and it should be carefully monitored to determine if it is working as expected. With this important caveat, we will describe some time-regulation strategies that have proven effective for others.

1. Setting regular study periods. By setting aside certain hours each day, studying requires less daily planning and becomes more habitual.

2. Setting realistic goals. Many students tend to underestimate the amount of time needed to complete an assignment and thus need to overestimate the time necessary until they are certain of their estimates.

3. Use a regular study area. Students are more time-efficient when they study in a place that is well-lighted, free from noise and distractions, and conducive to attention. Some students find a library a good place to study, whereas other students can create an effective study area at home.

4. Prioritize tasks. When students have many activities, they should prioritize those that need to be completed first. In general, it is better to study difficult subjects before studying easy ones because one's attention is usually better at the outset.

5. Learn to say no to distractions. When friends, siblings, or others want to talk instead of study or to skip studying entirely, students must be prepared to say no in a way that is not offensive.

6. Self-reward success. Students can improve their attention by making desirable activities contingent on completion of studying. This can include food treats, television, and seeing or talking with friends. The key is to ensure that the rewards are withheld until studying goals are met.

How to Select a Strategy

> It is important that students choose a strategy that can correct their specific deficiency and then monitor its implementation and effectiveness.

All approaches to study time planning and management begin with asking students to compare their process records with homework and quiz scores and to look for specific things that should be changed. Strategies for effecting those changes can come from a variety of sources. Students can (a) select a time-use strategy from their general knowledge of learning strategies; (b) devise their own strategy based on logical analyses of their particular procedural approach; or (c) consult with classmates, especially with competent students, or with their teacher regarding a course of action.

When Strategies Do Not Work

Not all strategies produce desired gains, especially at the outset. Breakdowns occur when performance is inadequately monitored, when strategies are improperly matched to goals or task, or when strategies are insufficiently implemented (e.g., when confusion in carrying them out occurs). Nonetheless, strategy breakdowns need not be considered failures but a source of further learning. As students reanalyze their data and see what part(s) of their strategy worked and what did not, understanding negative outcomes can prove to be an important stepping stone to success.

The purpose of this second phase of self-regulation is for students to discover their areas of deficiency and then to set process goals to overcome them. Our two students self-analyzed their data, noted deficiencies, and set self-correction goals.

During a small group follow-up, *Calvin* discovered that higher-achieving classmates spent, on average, an hour and 30 minutes on their arithmetic assignments. He concluded he would need to start his assignments earlier if he were to finish the problems before bedtime. He set a goal of 45 minutes per day but was uncertain how to juggle his afternoon habits to start studying earlier. Calvin's most pleasurable recreational activity was watching television. He loved to come home, switch on the set, sink into his favorite chair, and watch daily programs. Calvin was willing to adjust sports and any other afternoon activities but was not happy at the thought of missing his two favorite TV programs. His peers suggested that he need not discontinue them but could merely put them off on until after the homework problems were completed. He could videotape the two shows and view them after working on the problems. His self-reward strategy was to watch the videotapes only on the days when he spent 45 minutes on his arithmetic homework beginning at 5:00 pm.

Maria deduced from her process self-monitoring that she should work on her mathematics without social distractions. She also concluded that she needs to work for more than 45 minutes on this academic subject and decided to see if an hour was sufficient. Her strategy was to complete the assignments in a library that she passed on the way home because none of her friends spent time there.

STRATEGY IMPLEMENTATION AND MONITORING

The academic schedules of most schools encourage students to shift their time habits often during the course of a school year. Until they monitor exactly how they are spending their time, however, most students are not aware of the priorities they build into their time use. Unfortunately, most students wait until the last minute before

> Students rarely plan or manage their available time for studying but complete their academic assignments on a reactive basis.

studying for major tests or writing important papers.

Because students usually have little experience structuring their own time, it is important for the teacher to provide support as students begin to develop and implement strategic efforts to develop their time planning and management skills. Support can best be offered by helping students find concrete ways to adjust their schedules and by providing students enough opportunities to see the effects of their new strategic approaches. Let us see how Calvin and Maria fared in their strategic efforts.

Calvin met his arithmetic time goals on the first two days and watched the videotapes on both days. On the third and fourth days, he found himself distracted by one thing or another and did not get to his homework until the evening. He was able to spend only 30 minutes on his arithmetic those days. Although disappointed in not meeting his time goals, he maturely adhered to his self-reward strategy by not watching television. He received 8s on the two assignments he completed during his new time schedule, and 3s on the assignments he worked on late at night. He got a 6 on his arithmetic quiz, which disappointed him. His self-efficacy ratings for the two days when he failed to meet his time goals were 4 (i.e., $5 - 1 = 4$), indicating not very sure of getting even a 5. On the two days that he did meet his time goals, he felt absolutely sure he would earn at least a 6, so his self-efficacy scores for those days were 7 (i.e., $6 + 1 = 7$). He estimated his self-efficacy for the weekly quiz at 6, indicating he was quite sure of attaining a 6 (i.e., $6 + 0 = 6$), which in fact he did achieve.

Although *Maria* highly valued her standing among her peers, she vowed to improve her mathematics quiz scores. She was rigorous about working alone on the problems for an hour each afternoon, and using the library proved to be a good strategy. Initially, her homework grades suffered from the lack of help. She got a couple of 4s whereas she had earned 6s and 8s when working with her friends. This negative experience undermined her sense of self-efficacy for receiving even a 6 on the weekly quiz, lowering it to 5 ($6 - 1 = 5$) because she had to rely only on herself. In fact, she earned a 6.

STRATEGIC-OUTCOME MONITORING

As we have seen, the first effort to establish new habits is rarely a complete success. Students need to be given the opportunity to modify their initial approaches. As long as they continue to carefully monitor how they implement their new strategies, they are likely to see where refinement should take place. From the repeated opportunities to learn from their own strategic efforts, students can develop varied and unique time-management techniques.

It was clear from *Calvin*'s process records that his arithmetic performance improved when he met his time goals. Missing his television programs motivated him to put aside distractions and start his arithmetic homework at 5:00 pm and work for 45 minutes every day the following week. His homework score picked up to 5 that week, and his quiz self-efficacy score increased to 6 because from his past week's monitoring he saw that he could earn a 6 on the quiz if he met his studying goals. In fact, he did earn a 6 on the quiz.

The following week, Calvin decided to shoot for a higher score on the arithmetic quiz. Because he had trouble finishing the problems within the 45-minute study period, Calvin raised his time goal to 1 hour of homework a night. He reached his goal each day and earned an average score of 7 on his homework assignments and a 7 on the quiz. His average self-efficacy ratings for the weekly problems jumped to 8, indicating that he was absolutely sure he would get at least a 7 (i.e., 7 + 1 = 8), and he expected the same results on the weekly arithmetic quiz (self-efficacy = 8).

To raise his quiz score even higher, Calvin set his sights on adding additional time to review the difficult problems. He would review for a half-hour on Thursday evening and another half-hour on Friday morning. His strategy remained the same, to watch the videotapes only when he met all his time goals. Calvin's arithmetic homework scores rose to an average of 8 as a result of his increased study time. His self-efficacy rating also increased in anticipation of the time he would put in for review. He reported a self-efficacy rating of 9 for the weekly arithmetic quiz, indicating that he was absolutely sure he would get at least an 8 (i.e., 8 + 1 = 9). His confidence was well-placed because he did earn an 8 on the quiz. The most interesting development for Calvin was his interest in arithmetic. With his increasing success in his studying, he found himself asking more questions in class instead of daydreaming about his favorite TV programs.

Table 1 shows the processes involved as Calvin improved his time planning and management skills.

Table 1 | Calvin's Self-Regulated Development of Time Planning and Management Skills

	Week	Process/feedback/plan
Self-evaluation and monitoring	1	*Processes monitored*: Began arithmetic homework after 9 pm, worked 25 minutes daily *Feedback*: homework average = 2, quiz = 4, self-efficacy = 3
Planning and goal setting		*Goal*: Start assignments at 5 pm, increase time to 45 minutes daily *Strategy*: Watch videotapes only if goal is achieved
Strategy implementation and monitoring	2	*Processes monitored*: Met time goals 2 of 4 days, adhered to strategy all 4 days *Feedback*: Homework average = 5.5, quiz = 6, self-efficacy = 6
Strategic-outcome monitoring	3	*Processes monitored*: Met daily time goals all 4 days, adhered to strategy all 4 days *Feedback*: Homework average = 5.5, quiz = 6, self-efficacy = 6 *New goal*: Extend time to 1 hour
	4	*Processes monitored*: Met time goals all 4 days, adhered to strategy all 4 days *Feedback*: Homework average = 7, quiz = 7, self-efficacy = 8 *New goal*: Add 30 minutes for quiz review on Thursday and 30 minutes on Friday morning
	5	*Processes monitored*: Met time goals all 4 days, adhered to strategy all 4 days *Feedback*: Homework average = 8, quiz = 8, self-efficacy = 9

Maria continued to work math problems in the library, and her average homework score increased to 7. She was getting better at handling the problems on her own. She felt confident about her strategy, and her self-efficacy ratings rose to an average of 8, indicating that she was quite sure she would earn at least an 8 on the quiz (i.e., $8 + 0 = 8$), which she did. In spite of the evidence that her mathematical skills were improving, Maria was unhappy about her new time plan because she missed the social aspect of studying. So she decided to work at home some days once in a while so she could call a friend to compare answers on the telephone.

Unfortunately for Maria, this change ushered in some of her old habits. She only adhered to her strategy of going to the library on two days the following week. Her math homework scores declined to an average of 5. Her weekly quiz self-efficacy rating declined to 7, indicating she was no longer sure of earning an 8. She also lost the gain she had made on her quiz, which went back down to 6.

Maria was not willing to abandon her phone-socializing time, so she decided to give herself an extra incentive to stick to her library strategy. She wanted to raise her mathematics quiz score even more, so she decided to add additional review time. Maria planned to review for the quiz for a half-hour on Thursday with her friends and alone for another half-hour on Friday. A new strategy was added to help her meet these more demanding goals. She obtained her parents permission to invite her two best friends to her home for a slumber party on Friday night if she consistently met her time goals. This strategy actually improved her motivation. She did not mind studying alone in the library because it earned her two self-rewards: the evening phone conversation and her slumber party at the end of the week. Her math homework score increased to an average of 9, and her quiz self-efficacy ratings rose to 9, reflecting absolute confidence that she would get at least an 8 (i.e., $8 + 1 = 9$). She earned a 9 on the quiz and had a great time at her party.

	Week	Process/feedback/plan
Table 2 — Maria's Self-Regulated Development of Time Planning and Management Skills		
Self-evaluation and monitoring	1	*Processes monitored*: 45 minutes daily working with a friend *Feedback*: Arithmetic homework average = 7, quiz = 7, self-efficacy = 6
Planning and goal setting		*Goal*: Study alone for 1 hour *Strategy*: Go to library where friends do not hang out
Strategy implementation and monitoring	2	*Processes monitored*: Consistently adhered to strategy, consistently met time goal *Feedback*: Homework average = 5, quiz = 6, self-efficacy = 5
Strategic-outcome monitoring	3	*Processes monitored*: Consistently adhered to strategy, consistently met time goal *Feedback*: Homework average = 7, quiz = 8, self-efficacy = 8 *New goal*: Study 1 hour at home alone and review with friends on phone
	4	*Processes monitored*: Adhered to strategy 2 out of 4 days, met study time goal 2 out of 4 days, consistently met review time goal *Feedback*: Homework average = 5, quiz = 6, self-efficacy = 7 *New goal*: Add quiz review with friends for 30 minutes Thursday and alone for 30 minutes Friday *New strategy*: Have Friday slumber party if consistently meet all time goals for week
	5	*Processes monitored*: Consistently met all time goals, consistently adhered to strategy *Feedback*: Homework average = 9, quiz = 9, self-efficacy = 9

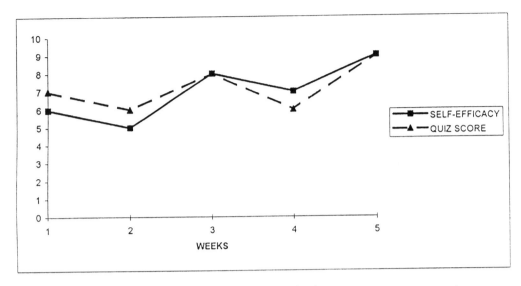

Figure 4 *Maria's plotted outcome scores by week of time management intervention.*

Table 2 shows the processes involved as Maria improved her time planning and management skills.

Maria's self-efficacy ratings and math quiz scores are depicted graphically in Figure 4.

SELF-EFFICACY PERCEPTIONS

> One of the greatest strengths of self-regulatory approaches to academic skill development is that they provide students with the opportunities to see how activities under their control can bring them rewarding feelings.

Just as students refine their strategies from self-monitored feedback, they also become more finely attuned to their feelings of efficacy. Perceptions of low self-efficacy point to precise areas where students need to apply further effort. Because they are guided accurately by dips in their feelings of capability, these students are able to self-correct their study behavior strategically without exposing themselves to adverse test results. Calvin found that his strategic efforts to manage his study time gave him a better feeling of self-worth, and he sensed that his teacher's estimation of him rose because he was contributing to class discussions.

Feelings of self-confidence are very motivating to students who have not enjoyed many successes in school. Students are more apt to take responsibility for their learning when they realize that they are capable of achieving on their own.

PERSONAL AND SOCIAL BENEFITS OF TIME PLANNING AND MANAGEMENT

Our student examples show that by attending to specific details of the way they use their time for studying, they found unique ways to address their deficits and to develop their strengths. Through the use of self-regulatory techniques to develop their time planning and management, these students enhanced their grasp of the course mate-rial, their quiz scores, and their self-efficacy perceptions. But will Calvin and Maria be the only ones to benefit from these gains? Their classmates experiencing time-management problems may be encouraged vicariously by Calvin's and Maria's improvement to try corresponding strategies for their own betterment. Also, small group and whole class discussions in their mathematics classes will be invigorated by the addition of students who now feel prepared to participate. Calvin's and Maria's teachers will be less concerned that these students will be unprepared to participate in class and perform up to their potential on tests.

Teachers will be surprised at what pupils can discover from their time-use data. Some students will find that they are unaware of how much time they waste, underestimate the time they need to complete assignments, and are less efficient with time than they imagined. Other youngsters will learn that proper time management requires planning and self-discipline but that the results are worth the effort—in attaining greater learning, higher scores, and increased self-efficacy.

To assist you in implementing this self-regulatory cycle for students' time planning and management, we have provided a checklist in Exhibit 2.

EXHIBIT 2	Teacher's Checklist for Developing Students' Time Management Skills

1. Planning
   ____ Plan time management activities (See Implementation, below) lasting 5 weeks so that they mesh coherently with the curriculum
   ____ Make sure that time management assignments are equal in length and difficulty
2. Implementation
   Week 1
   ____ Introduce concept of self-efficacy and how to calculate it
   ____ Give students practice using their regular time management techniques (to obtain "baseline" data)
   Weeks 2–5
   ____ Give daily reading assignments (prepared, above) that elicit time management skills
   ____ Prepare and administer 10-question quizzes at end of each week (for testing comprehension of material and as a basis for students' self-efficacy judgments)
   ____ Prepare adequate supply of time management charts similar to that shown in Exhibit 1
   ____ Explain how to record data on the time management chart
   ____ Model goal setting and strategy selection in early weeks
   ____ Demonstrate how to graph self-efficacy and quiz scores
   ____ Provide small or peer group time in class to permit students to evaluate together their own and others' strategies and to refine them (weekly)
   ____ Observe small or peer groups to obtain insights into which strategies work and why (weekly)
   ____ Use information gathered from observing groups as a springboard for brief whole-class discussions on strategy selection and refinement (weekly)
   ____ Keep records of students' self-efficacy and quiz scores
   ____ Review students' graphed data after 3–4 weeks
   ____ Determine whether there is congruence between self-efficacy and quiz scores for each student. If not, data may indicate the need for teacher's attention to "stand out" students (either overly high or low in perceived self-efficacy, given quiz results)
3. Follow-up
   ____ Plan and implement time management follow-up activities for some time later in the course (to reinforce prior time management learning and to generalize this learning to other assignments or tasks)

1 In which aspects of study time planning and management will your students need the most help?

2 Which sections of the Study Time Self-Monitoring Form will be most helpful for your students? Are there any sections of the form you might you wish to change, and if so, how they could be adapted?

3 What problems do you anticipate in helping your students self-monitor their use of academic study time?

4 Describe the time planning and management strategies that will be most helpful to your students and explain why the strategies could help.

SUGGESTED READINGS

Ellis, D. (1994). *Becoming a master student.* Rapid City, SD: College Survival.

Zimmerman, B. J., Greenberg, D., & Weinstein, C. E. (1994). Self-regulating academic study time: A strategy approach. In D. H. Schunk & B. J. Zimmerman (Eds.), *Self-regulation of learning and performance: Issues and educational applications* (pp. 181–199) Hillsdale, NJ: Erlbaum.

goal 3

Developing Text Comprehension
and Summarization Skills

Because much school learning is gained through reading of textual material, students must become proficient in understanding text. Teachers can bring text-comprehension skills under self-regulatory control by highlighting the processes students use when they read and summarize text.

The four components of the self-regulatory model—self-evaluation, goal setting and strategic planning, strategy implementation and refinement, and strategic-outcome monitoring—can be incorporated into a 5-week unit within the framework of typical instructional practices. What is needed is for teachers to recast the use of class time that they would ordinarily spend on homework review. Time that is normally spent discussing homework answers with the class can be shifted to peer scoring of homework summaries from model summaries developed by the teacher. These daily-summarization scores can be compared with weekly quiz outcomes to show the students how effective summaries lead to improved test outcomes. Thus, teachers can use homework review time as an opportunity to help students interpret text strategically, to attend to students' efforts to find ways to develop their skills, and to suggest areas where students can concentrate their efforts as they refine their text-summarization skills.

To some educators, text comprehension and text summarization are two discrete skills: the first referring to reading and parsing of meaning from an assigned reading, and the second to recording efficiently and accurately the important ideas that were gleaned. However, the basic skills needed for the first task are needed also for the second: locating main ideas and themes, extracting supporting facts, and applying acquired knowledge. As students develop these two self-regulatory skills, teachers can expect them to display greater conceptual understanding of the material and to provide more objective information in support of their reasoning.

SELF-EVALUATION AND MONITORING

Opportunities for self-regulation are presented through homework assignments when students read and summarize textual passages followed by a quiz at the end of the week based on these readings. It should be evident that this exercise differs from the format of the previous self-regulatory exercise only insofar as student-prepared summaries take the place of students answering teacher-prepared questions. As in the previous exercise, the reading assignments and quizzes should be roughly equivalent in scope, length, and difficulty, so that daily progress can be inferred without ambiguity. One-half of the class period is required at the beginning of the first week of this exercise for the teacher to introduce the summarization process. Then the teacher asks students to take notes or to highlight the text that will be assigned during this self-regulatory exercise and to bring their summaries to class for peer scoring. If the teacher prepares model summaries of the text passages, enumerating the main ideas, the students may compare their peers' summaries to it and assign scores on the basis of the degree of correspondence. When recording the peer-assigned scores on the students' summaries, teachers will be able to check how well peers were able to follow the grading criteria. By delegating scoring to peers, teachers give students the opportunity to observe and objectively assess another student's performance. In so doing, this exercise should improve their own self-assessment skills.

The self-regulatory aspect of this exercise begins with students monitoring the processes they use when they summarize text passages. They may use a simple form such as the one in Exhibit 3. This form allows students a view of how much time is spent processing text passages of varying lengths, how many ideas they extract into summaries, how many of those summary ideas they highlight (indicating some review of their summaries), and how many sentences they generate to encapsulate the themes of the passage.

Assume once again that the weekly quizzes consist of 10 questions and are scored with a point for every correct answer. As was illustrated earlier, self-efficacy is defined as the estimated score on homework or quizzes after the point adjustment on the basis of the students' confidence in their answer.

During the first week, students usually begin to appreciate the selective processes they need to identify necessary and sufficient information from textual readings. Initially, summarization responsibilities may slow down students' reading time, but as this skill is mastered, their

EXHIBIT 3			Text Comprehension and Summarization Self-Monitoring Form			
Date	Time Spent	No. of Pages in Text	No. of Main Ideas Summarized	No. of Summaries Highlighted	No. of Theme Sentences Written	Self-Efficacy

time requirements decrease. Teachers can monitor their students' progress over the 5-week module by asking them to report their average self-efficacy rating on the final homework assignment for the week.

Let us examine what Calvin and Maria discovered about the way they handled their science reading assignments.

Calvin usually receives Ds in science, often as "gifts" from his teachers. He does not like science and considers the class his worst. He is a poor reader who rarely completes homework assignments. Calvin reads only the main headings of text assignments and sometimes glances at the first paragraph within a new heading. He usually does not take notes as he reads. During class discussions, Calvin avoids talking, and when called on, he speaks in generalities. He spent about a minute per page of text and copied a sentence or two from the first paragraphs following the main headings to produce the summaries the teacher had requested, and he counted these as main ideas. Exhibit 4 shows the text passage that Calvin's teacher assigned him to summarize. Figure 5 presents Calvin's first effort. His score for his summaries averaged 2, indicating that he had failed to capture many of the ideas in the teacher's model summaries, but his summaries were better on the pages where he spent slightly more time. Calvin's self-efficacy rating was 6, indicating he had been very sure of getting a 6 (i.e., $6 + 0 = 6$). In fact, he did more poorly on the quiz with a 4.

Maria has averaged a C grade in science throughout the school year. She spent 10 minutes reading and taking brief notes on each page of the text, and she captured a few main ideas. She neither reviewed her

EXHIBIT 4 Textual Material Assigned for Calvin to Summarize.

An Insidious Enemy

Drought is an insidious enemy. It sneaks up on us. Unlike such other weather dangers as hurricanes, tornadoes, and electrical storms, it does not strike in a sudden, roaring fury and last for just minutes or hours. Rather, it comes quietly in the cheerful guise of clear, sunny skies and then remains to work its damage just as quietly over a period of weeks, months, or even years. Its stealth can delude us into making tragic errors.

At first, because we are enjoying the fine weather, we often do not realize that drought is in our midst until it inflicts so much damage that it can no longer be ignored. Once we do recognize its presence, we often make the mistake of thinking it cannot possibly hang about much longer. Rain will often contribute to the harm being done. We delay too long in enacting measures that will help us conserve our dwindling supply of water.

All the while, rivers, streams, and wells—no longer replenished by rain and melting snow—begin to run dry. Likewise, the water that nature keeps stored in the group is lost through evaporation. The soil turns dry and hard under a coating of dust. Plants wither and die. Animals begin to die of thirst and—since there is no longer enough plant life on which to feed—starvation. Given sufficient time to run completely out of water, we, too, face death.[1]

As matters worsen, other dangers appear. The weather produces dry conditions that make forest and grass fires a daily threat. The dryness can generate winds that will send the parched soil whipping into the air in blinding dust storms. These storms—nicknamed "black blizzards" and "dusters"—are a particular menace in farm areas where topsoil has been loosened by years of plowing. Some of the worst occurred during the drought that plagued the American Great Plains in the 1930s. These storms carried dust thousands of feet into the air and turned day into night for hours at a time. One such black blizzard sent clouds of dust billowing eastward beyond New York City and out over the Atlantic Ocean.

Excerpted from *Drought*, by E. F. Dolen, pp. 11–14. Copyright 1990 by Franklin Watts. Reprinted by permission.

[1] Humans need to consume about $2\frac{1}{2}$ quarts (2.3 l) of water per day. We take in about $1\frac{1}{2}$ (1.4 l) from the liquids we drink, with the remaining quart being provided by the water content in our foods. Our bodies are made up of about 95 to 98 percent water. This works out to about 30 quarts (28 l) or 114 pounds (51.3 kg) if you're a young person weighing 120 pounds (54 kg). Lose as little as 13 percent of that body water and your life is endangered.

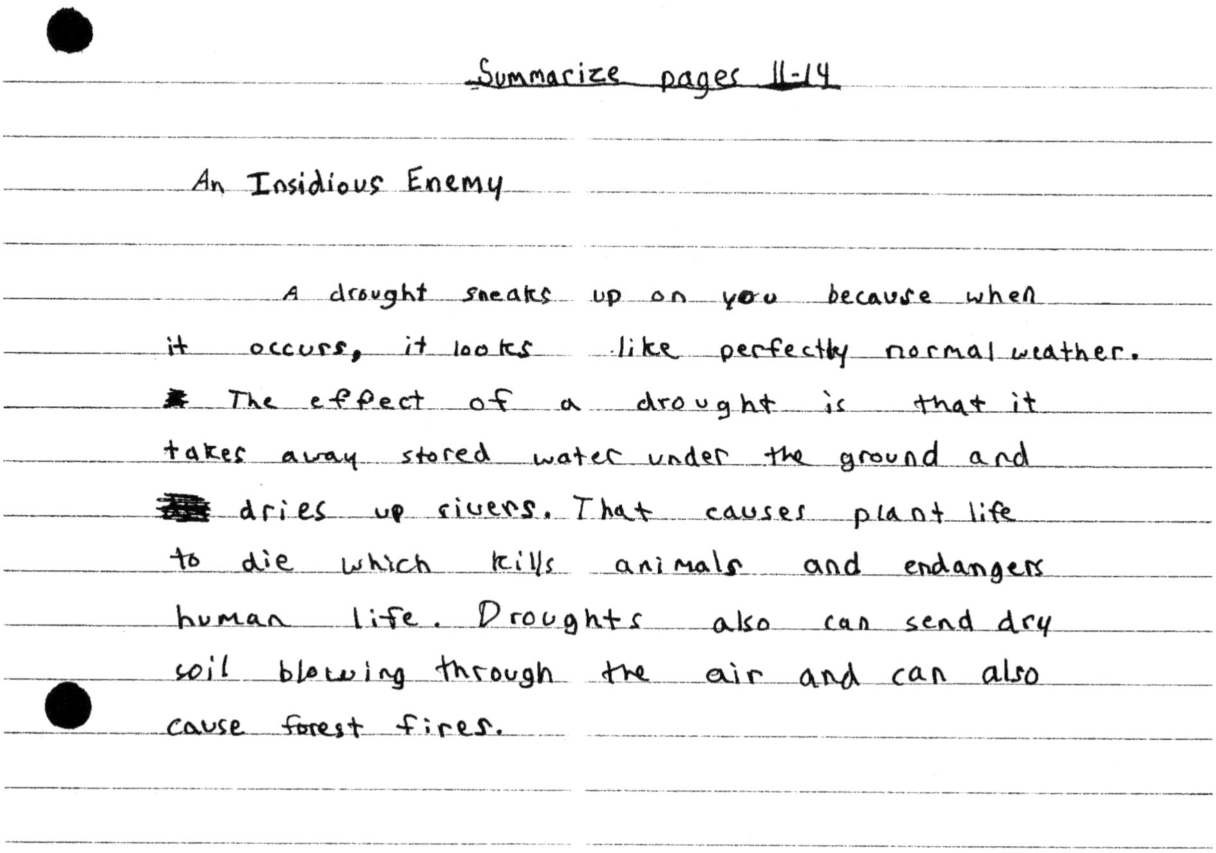

An Insidious Enemy

A drought sneaks up on you because when it occurs, it looks like perfectly normal weather. The effect of a drought is that it takes away stored water under the ground and dries up rivers. That causes plant life to die which kills animals and endangers human life. Droughts also can send dry soil blowing through the air and can also cause forest fires.

Figure 5 *Calvin's complete summary of this material about drought.*

summaries nor generated sentences that summarized the entire passages. As a result, her summaries scored only 5, and she earned a 5 on the quiz. Her self-efficacy rating had been a cautious 4, indicating she was not very sure of receiving an 5 on her summary (i.e., 5 − 1 = 4).

GOAL SETTING AND STRATEGIC PLANNING

A half-period at the beginning of the second week is allocated to help students evaluate their text-summarization processes. The teacher can encourage them to examine the dimensions they monitored, for example, how long they spent per page of text, how many main ideas they captured, how much text they highlighted, and how many theme sentences they generated. The aim is for students to set specific process goals for developing their summarization skills.

Selected Reading Comprehension and Summarization Strategies

Listed below are some commonly used strategies to understand textual material, especially if it is complex. The list is not suggested to be inclusive but merely illustrative of strategies that have been effective. Students may wish to refer to other sources (see *Suggested Readings*) or to develop their own strategies. As we mentioned with regard to time planning and management, no strategy is universally effective, but each one has specific effects and works well in certain contexts. Therefore, each strategy should be chosen only when it is appropriate, and it should be carefully monitored to determine if it is actually working. With this stipulation in mind, we will describe a number of strategies that might be considered.

1. Clarifying difficulties encountered. Slowing down to read more carefully and checking back and rereading when text meaning is unclear.

2. Self-questioning. Questions that students can ask themselves to understand the material at a deeper level, such as "Why is that true?"

3. Predicting what will come next. Stopping to anticipate what the author will say or conclude next before reading a text passage.

4. Finding the main idea. Analyzing passages, such as a paragraph, and identifying the main idea that is being discussed.

5. Summarization. Paring down passages to their core

meaning by eliminating trivial or redundant information, substituting superordinate terms for lists of items, integrating a series of events with a superordinate action term, and inventing a topic sentence.

6. Relating text to prior knowledge. Relating ideas in text to previously stored information, often in the form of analogies, examples, extensions, and comparisons.

Choosing Appropriate Comprehension and Summarization Strategies

Students begin to individualize their skill development during this second phase of self-regulation. The monitoring form that guided their initial focus on text summarization processes provides the basis for their individualized planning. Let us see the decisions our illustrative students made in response to their precise monitoring of their text-summarization processes.

> *Calvin's* conclusion that he did poorly in science because "he did not like it" was disconfirmed by his self-records that revealed his lack of preparation for the course. Students with higher grades had longer notes. His monitoring sheets helped him to see something that no teacher's comments had ever made clear—that the grades he earned in science were directly tied to the quality of his notes. He decided to set his goals much higher for his notes because he wanted to pass the quizzes. He would try and spend more time on every page he read, and he would try and extract two or three main ideas in his notes. However, he did not plan to try to summarize his notes into themes, and so he did not monitor those processes. His strategy was to read each paragraph and copy the one sentence that best captured its meaning.
>
> *Maria* wanted to make sure that she

not only captured the meaning of the text passages but her notes also would serve as an overview of each night's readings. She decided to create theme sentences to summarize the sections of the science book. Her strategy would be twofold. She would pose a question to herself after reading every three or four paragraphs, "Why were those ideas true?" In addition, she would review the entire summary for a section of the book and highlight the important trends. With these two methods, she hoped to be able to understand the thematic content of the science readings.

STRATEGY IMPLEMENTATION AND MONITORING

Students can lose self-confidence if they expect immediate improvements in their outcomes; however, they will experience increases in their self-efficacy if the teacher stresses the importance of mastering their new strategies.

Students need to conscientiously apply their new strategies. This may be daunting if they have habitually followed other practices for a long time. The best way to ensure that they are actually engaging in the new effort is for them to self-monitor. In most cases, students will simply be able to use the same form to monitor their strategy implementation that they used to initially evaluate their comprehension and summarization processes. The measure of students' success during this phase of self-regulation is not how much their performance improves but how well they apply their new strategies. It is important for teachers to support student efforts to improve by focusing rigorously on learning processes, not outcomes.

Calvin followed his strategy only once during the next 4 days. It was very difficult for him to find a single sentence that captured the meaning of an entire paragraph in the science book. Although he spent slightly more time per page, he counted only five main ideas per page. He had evidently not been able to select the right sentences because he was still earning only 4s for his summaries, and he once again did poorly on the quiz with a 4. His self-efficacy rating was accurate at 4, reflecting that he was unsure about attaining a 5 (i.e., $5 - 1 = 4$).

Maria consistently followed her strategy. While she was reading, she asked herself to justify the reasons for the ideas presented. When she had finished reading the assigned science material, she reviewed her summaries and highlighted five lines. She was able to generate three sentences to capture the theme. Her summaries now earned her 8s, and she scored another 8 on the quiz. Her self-efficacy ratings rose to 8, reflecting her near certainty at being able to score 8 on the quiz (i.e., $8 + 0 = 8$).

STRATEGIC-OUTCOME MONITORING

As long as students maintain their effort to apply their strategies conscientiously, they will find ways to overcome obstacles. The self-regulatory approach assumes neither that there is a single strategy that will work for all students nor that a single implementation effort will work for any student. Strategies are not magic. If they were, the job of educators would be simple indeed. A strategy becomes powerful only if its implementation is monitored and evaluated. On evaluation, students refine their strategies by focusing on dimensions of their skilled efforts needing improvement.

Calvin still was unable to use the sentence-selection strategy consistently during the second week, and the results showed. His scores for his summaries and on the quiz remained unchanged, as did his self-efficacy rating for the science quiz. His teacher noted the unchanging pattern and suggested that he may have to add another component to his summarization strategy. The teacher suggested that after reading each paragraph, Calvin describe its meaning and then try to find a sentence in the paragraph that answers that question.

This extra step paid off. Calvin was able to consistently apply the strategy in the following week, and he was able to capture 10 main ideas per summary. His summary scores averaged 4, and his quiz score improved to 5, still a poor grade. As he saw that he was able to get more involved through self-questioning, Calvin's self-efficacy rating increased to 5, indicating he was quite sure of getting at least a 5 (i.e., $5 + 0 = 5$). From class discussions about summarization strategies, he learned that the first and last sentences of paragraphs tended to be thematic, so he decided to refine his strategy again by focusing on the first and last sentences of each paragraph to answer his question about the meaning of paragraph.

Calvin spent more time summarizing each page in the science book the following week, and he captured 15 main ideas, sometimes by finding them in the first or last sentence, and sometimes by writing one himself. His practice in summarizing during the previous month had helped him discover the point of each paragraph, and focusing on the first and last sentences helped select the one that best captured the main point. Exhibit 5 and Figure 6 present a portion of the text that Calvin was assigned to summarize and a page from his

EXHIBIT 5	Textual Material for Calvin to Summarize after His Comprehension and Summarization Skills Improved.

Cloud Seeding. The process became known as cloud seeding, and the Soviet Union quickly put it to use—but not against drought. The enemy, rather, was the hailstorms that so often attacked the Ukraine, the nation's great wheat-growing area. When hailstones pelted the earth, they could destroy a wheat crop in minutes. Hailstones are chunks of ice that form in especially turbulent clouds. The Soviets adopted, and still use, the practice of firing chemically filled artillery shells and rockets into clouds to turn the hailstones into rain.

The strategy works this way. On reaching a certain height, the shells explode and spew their cargoes of dry ice or silver iodide throughout the clouds. The water droplets in the clouds collect on the arriving crystals rather than on the chunks of ice that are forming as hailstones. The result is that the stones are reduced in size or, in some instances, eliminated altogether. The water droplets then fall principally as rain.[1]

Ever since trying this strategy, Soviet scientists have reported that it has produced successful results. They claim it has reduced hail damage to grapes and other crops by as much as 60 to 90 percent.

Cloud Seeding: A Real Help? When cloud seeding was first developed, many people thought that it was the weapon that would finally put an end to drought. All that had to be done to bring rain was to release the chemicals from aircraft or send them up from the ground in the heat created by generators. But such has not proved to be the case. While there is no doubt that the process works, it has certain limitations and has triggered a number of questions about its effectiveness.

Its most serious limitation in the fight against drought stems from two basic facts. First, as its very name makes clear, clouds must be present before the technique can be employed. Second, not all clouds bear rain; experiments have shown that seeding will not work unless the clouds on the scene are capable of bringing rain. Unfortunately, drought is usually present under cloudless skies or under what are called fair-weather clouds—clouds that, because of their content and the surrounding atmospheric conditions, cannot produce rain. In both these instances, seeding is a helpless tool.

Excerpted from *Drought*, by E. F. Dolen, pp. 104–106. Copyright 1990 by Franklin Watts. Reprinted by permission.

[1] Long before these firings, the Soviets had been shooting regular artillery shells into the skies above the Ukraine to thwart the hailstorms, acting on the belief that cloudbursts do indeed follow battles.

Summ. P 104-107

Cloud Seeding

1. The Soviet Union, in order to stop hailstorms
   from destroying wheat crops in the Ukraine,
   used the process of cloud seeding.
   - hailstones are chunks of ice that are
     very destructive.
   - the Soviets shot chemical filled rockets and
     shells up into the clouds.
2. The strategy works this way.
   - the water droplets collect on the chemicals
     instead of on the hailstones.
3. The Soviets claim that cloud seeding reduces
   the amount of damage by 60-90 percent.

Cloud Seeding: a Real Help?
1. There is no doubt that the process works
   but there are many questions about its
   effectiveness.
2. Its most serious limitation stems from two facts.
   - clouds must be present.
   - the clouds must bear rain.
   - unfortunately drout usually ~~occurs~~ occurs under
     ~~~~ cloudless skies

Figure 6 *The first page of Calvin's summary of this material on "Cloud Seeding."*

summary. His summary scores remained at 6, a good score for him, and he improved on his quiz results to a 6. Calvin had felt quite sure that he would get at least a 6 on the quiz, which was reflected in his self-efficacy ratings of 6 (i.e., 6 + 0 = 6).

Table 3 shows the processes involved as Calvin improved his text summarization and processing skills.

Maria consistently applied her strategy for science readings during the second week. She captured 15 main ideas, highlighted five lines of her summaries, and wrote three theme sentences. She scored a perfect score on her summaries but again got an 8 on the quiz. Her self-efficacy ratings had remained the same at 8. Maria decided that she would try and achieve a perfect score on the science quiz, and she would adjust her strategy to do so. She wanted to get a better idea of the themes of the passage, so after reading three or four paragraphs and asking herself about them, she would try and predict what direction the reading would then take.

Maria consistently followed her new strategy. Her summaries captured 15 main ideas, she highlighted 10 lines of those summaries, and she generated 10 theme sentences, a far greater conceptual overview of the reading. Her scores for the summaries remained perfect at 10, and her self-efficacy ratings rose to 9, indicating that she was not very sure she would get a perfect score on the quiz (i.e., 10 − 1 = 9). Her quiz score in science rose to only 9, so Maria refined her strategy further. She would try to link the material she was about to read to familiar frameworks by asking herself, "What do I already know about this or related topics?"

Table 3

Calvin's Self-Regulated Development of Text Comprehension and Summarization Skills

	Week	Process/feedback/plan
Self-evaluation and monitoring	1	*Processes monitored*: Average per page in science book: number of main ideas = 3, number of lines highlighted = 0, number of theme sentences = 0 *Feedback*: Summaries average = 2, quiz = 4, self-efficacy = 6
Planning and goal setting		*Goal*: Identify 15 main ideas per page in science book *Strategy*: Read each paragraph, copy the one sentence that best summarizes the meaning of the paragraph, or write a sentence to summarize the paragraph
Strategy implementation and monitoring	2	*Processes monitored*: Followed strategy 1 out of 4 days, average number of main ideas = 5 per page *Feedback*: Summaries average = 4, quiz = 4, self-efficacy = 4
Strategic outcome monitoring	3	*Processes monitored*: Followed strategy 2 out of 4 days, average number of main ideas = 6 *Feedback*: Summaries average = 4, quiz = 4, self-efficacy = 4 *New strategy*: Read a paragraph, ask myself, "What was that paragraph about?" Find a sentence in the paragraph that answers that question
	4	*Processes monitored*: Consistently followed strategy, average number of main ideas = 10 *Feedback*: Summaries average = 4, quiz = 5, self-efficacy = 5 *New strategy*: Focus on first and last sentence of paragraph
	5	*Processes monitored*: Consistently followed strategy, number of main ideas per page = 15 *Feedback*: Summaries average = 6, quiz = 6, self-efficacy = 6

Again, Maria consistently followed her strategy and saw a huge increase in her conceptual understanding of the material when she generated 15 theme sentences of the material. Her self-efficacy ratings rose to 10, reflecting her near certainty that her complex strategy of self-questioning and summarizing would enable her to earn a 10 on the quiz (i.e., 10 + 0 = 10), which it did.

Table 4 shows the processes involved as Maria improved her text summarization and processing skills.

SELF-EFFICACY PERCEPTIONS

Perceptions of low self-efficacy are clues to the precise areas where students need to apply further effort, and from this information, students can decide how to modify their strategies to make them more effective. Conversely, students begin to recognize which aspects of their efforts increase their feelings of confidence, such as Calvin's strategy for locating the main idea. These feelings of self-confidence are especially rewarding to him because he had not enjoyed many successes in school. Self-regulatory approaches to skill development provide students with concrete opportunities to see how strategies can improve their academic functioning. When they can witness the power of their learning methods personally, they are much more inclined to take responsibility for their learning.

> By rating their self-efficacy, students become more finely attuned to the role that judgments of capability can play in guiding their efforts.

To assist you in implementing this self-regulatory cycle for students' text summarization and processing, we have provided a checklist in Exhibit 6.

	Week	Process/feedback/plan
		Table 4 — Maria's Self-Regulated Development of Text Comprehension and Summarization Skills
Self-evaluation and monitoring	1	*Processes monitored*: Per page average number of main ideas in science = 15, number of lines highlighted = 0, number of theme sentences = 0 *Feedback*: Summaries average = 5, quiz = 5, self-efficacy = 4
Planning and goal setting		*Goal*: Create theme sentences to summarize the entire science reading *Strategy*: pose question every 3 or 4 paragraphs "Why were those ideas true?" Review the entire summary
Strategy implementation and monitoring	2	*Processes monitored*: Consistently followed strategy, number of main ideas = 15, number of lines highlighted = 5, number of theme sentences = 3 *Feedback*: Summaries average = 8, quiz = 8, self-efficacy = 8
Strategic outcome monitoring	3	*Processes monitored*: Consistently followed strategy, average number of main ideas = 15, number of lines highlighted = 5, number of theme sentences = 5 *Feedback*: Summaries average = 10, quiz = 8, self-efficacy = 8 *New goal*: Raise quiz average to 10 *New strategy*: Following self-question, predict what would follow
	4	*Processes monitored*: Consistently followed strategy, number of main ideas = 15, number of lines highlighted = 10, number of theme sentences = 10 *Feedback*: Summaries average = 10, quiz = 9, self-efficacy = 9 *New strategy*: Begin by self-questioning, "What do I already know about this or related topics?"
	5	*Processes monitored*: Consistently followed strategy, number of main ideas = 15, number of lines highlighted = 10, number of theme sentences = 15

EXHIBIT 6 **Teacher's Checklist for Developing Students' Text Comprehension and Summarization Skills**

1. Planning
   ____ Plan text comprehension and summarization activities (see Implementation, below) lasting 5 weeks so that they mesh well with the curriculum
   ____ Make sure that text comprehension and summarization assignments are equal in length and difficulty
2. Implementation
   Week 1
   ____ Review concept of self-efficacy and how to calculate it
   ____ Give students practice with their regular text comprehension and summarization techniques (to obtain "baseline" data)
   Weeks 2–5
   ____ Give daily reading assignments that elicit text comprehension and summarization skills
   ____ Prepare and administer 10-question quizzes at end of each week (for testing comprehension of material and as basis for students' self-efficacy judgments)
   ____ Prepare adequate supply of a reading comprehension and summarization chart similar to that shown in Exhibit 2.
   ____ Demonstrate (or model) extracting main ideas and theme sentences from reading selections that contain main ideas and themes
   ____ Provide small or peer group time in class to permit students to evaluate together their own and others' strategies and to refine them (weekly)
   ____ Observe small or peer groups to obtain insights into which strategies work and why (weekly)
   ____ Use information gathered from observing groups as a springboard for brief whole-class discussions on strategy selection and refinement (weekly)
   ____ Demonstrate how to graph text comprehension and summarization and quiz score data
   ____ Keep records of students' text summarization and comprehension and quiz scores.
   ____ Review students graphed data after 3–4 weeks
   ____ Determine whether there is congruence between self-efficacy and quiz scores for each student. If not, data may indicate the need for teacher's attention to "stand out" students (either overly high or low in perceived self-efficacy, given quiz results)
3. Follow-up
   ____ Plan and implement text comprehension and summarization follow-up activities for some time later in the course (to reinforce prior text comprehension and summarization learning and to generalize this learning to other assignments or tasks)

1 In which aspects of reading comprehension and summarization will your students need the most help?

2 Which sections of the Reading Comprehension and Summarization Self-Monitoring Form will be most helpful for your students? Are there any sections of the form you might you wish to change, and if so, how could they be adapted?

3 What problems do you anticipate in helping your students self-monitor their reading comprehension and summarization?

4 Describe the reading comprehension and summarization strategies that will be most helpful to your students and explain why the strategies could help.

SELECTED READINGS

Block, C. C. (1993). Strategy instruction in a literature-based reading program. *Elementary School Journal, 94,* 136–151.

Pressley, M., Symons, S., McGoldrick, J. A., & Snyder, B. (1995). Reading comprehension strategies. In M. Pressley, V. Woloshyn, J. Burkell, T. Cariglia-Bull, L. Lysynchuk, J.A. McGoldrick, B. Schneider, B.L. Snyder, & S. Symons (Eds.), *Cognitive strategy instruction that really improves children's academic performance* (2nd ed., pp. 57–100). Cambridge, MA: Brookline Books.

Symons, S., Richards, C. & Green, C. (1995). Cognitive strategies for reading comprehension. In E. Wood, V. E. Woloshyn, & Willoughby, T. (Eds.), *Cognitive strategy instruction for middle and high schools* (pp. 66–87). Cambridge, MA: Brookline Books.

goal 4

Developing Classroom
Note-Taking Skills

Self-regulatory development of classroom note-taking skills is a complex activity involving listening, analyzing, selecting, and writing. We have divided note taking into two basic operations, recording and revision, although both are vital to the production and use of high-quality notes. Each of these components involves a variety of subskills that bear on the production of accurate and effective notes. Recording strategies are designed to improve the retrieval of information for later review, whereas revision strategies are used to facilitate memorization. Revision is essential for effective recall because it involves reorganizing and rewriting notes in some logical order. Continuing revisions during the reviewing process for a test can help students further assimilate the material.

> The strategies that students use to record and revise their notes can greatly affect their grasp of the subject matter and their performance on tests and quizzes.

The teacher prepares for this self-regulatory exercise by creating outlines of his or her presentations and short weekly quizzes covering that content. Students will exchange their notes with their peers, compare their peers' class notes against the teacher's outlines, and score them for thoroughness and organization. Class time that is normally planned for homework review can be devoted to this self-regulatory exercise. In the first weeks, the teacher needs to prepare exemplary outline notes for every class on the basis of the lesson plan. As this exercise unfolds, teachers can ask the students to work in small peer groups to develop model outlines to score each other's notes. At the end of the week, the teacher administers the quiz and asks the students to score one another's efforts. If any students' self-efficacy ratings are at odds with their test results, they should be targeted by the teacher for special assistance.

SELF-EVALUATION AND MONITORING

To accurately self-evaluate their note taking, most students need to self-monitor this activity over some period of time. The monitoring form presented in Exhibit 7 will help students identify and analyze important elements of this process. This form should be completed after class so that it does not interfere with the process of note-taking. The

EXHIBIT 7	Note-Taking Self-Monitoring Form				
Date	Main Ideas	Supporting Facts	Lists	Revisions	Self-efficacy

form requires students to count the number of main ideas, supporting facts, and lists of points that they recorded, as well as any revisions (i.e. rewriting of the notes).

Assume once again that the weekly quizzes consist of 10 questions and are scored with a point for every correct answer. As was illustrated earlier, self-efficacy is defined as the estimated score on homework or quizzes after the point adjustment on the basis of the students' confidence in their answer.

During this first week, students may be expected to discern some general features of note-taking, for example, they may begin to appreciate only that they need to take notes on the important details of content and that following class their notes should be reorganized in some way. We will consider two students who reported differing note-taking patterns.

> *Calvin* has seldom taken notes during social studies class. He assumes the same information is in the book and that only students who can't understand the material need to take notes. But his recent success in taking summary notes from his science book made him realize that similar benefits might be expected from classroom note-taking efforts. Furthermore, Calvin's teacher has begun collecting the students' notes and quizzing them on their recall and understanding of social studies lectures and discussions. Calvin began to take notes, but he lacked a strategy, so his notes were meager and fragmentary. His analysis revealed only one main idea and two supporting facts but no lists or revisions. He earned only a 3 for his notes and a 3 on the quiz. His self-efficacy rating was 5, indicating that he optimistically hoped to earn at least an 6 (i.e., 6 − 1 = 5).
>
> *Maria* considers herself a capable history student despite the fact that her classroom notes leave a lot to be desired.

Inspection of her class notes revealed an incomplete record of her teacher's introduction of a topic, followed by considerable disarray in her coverage of the topic itself. Maria captured some important ideas, but there were many gaps between them. Her notes showed no identification of key terms and no underlining or highlighting of important ideas. Figure 7 presents Maria's notes from this lecture. She counted only three main ideas, seven supporting facts, a single list, and no revisions. Her notes were scored only 5, indicating neither completeness nor organization. She earned a 6 on the quiz. Her self-efficacy rating was 5, reflecting her lack of certainty of scoring a 6 on the quiz (i.e., $6 - 1 = 5$).

GOAL SETTING AND STRATEGIC PLANNING

The strategies available for developing note-taking skills address either recording, revision, or both functions. During recording, students attempt to capture the essential information from classroom work: main ideas, supporting facts and examples, summary lists, and connections between concepts. During revision, students reorganize their notes in either outline form or according to another method that is meaningful to the student and appropriate to the material (e.g., tables, matrices, and tree diagrams).

Selected Note-Taking Strategies

Listed below are some commonly used strategies to take notes during a teacher s lectures and revise them afterward. The list is not suggested to be exhaustive but merely illustrative of strategies that have been effective. In addition, students may wish to refer to other sources (see *Suggested Readings*) or to develop their own strategies. Each strategy should be chosen when it is most appropriate, and it should

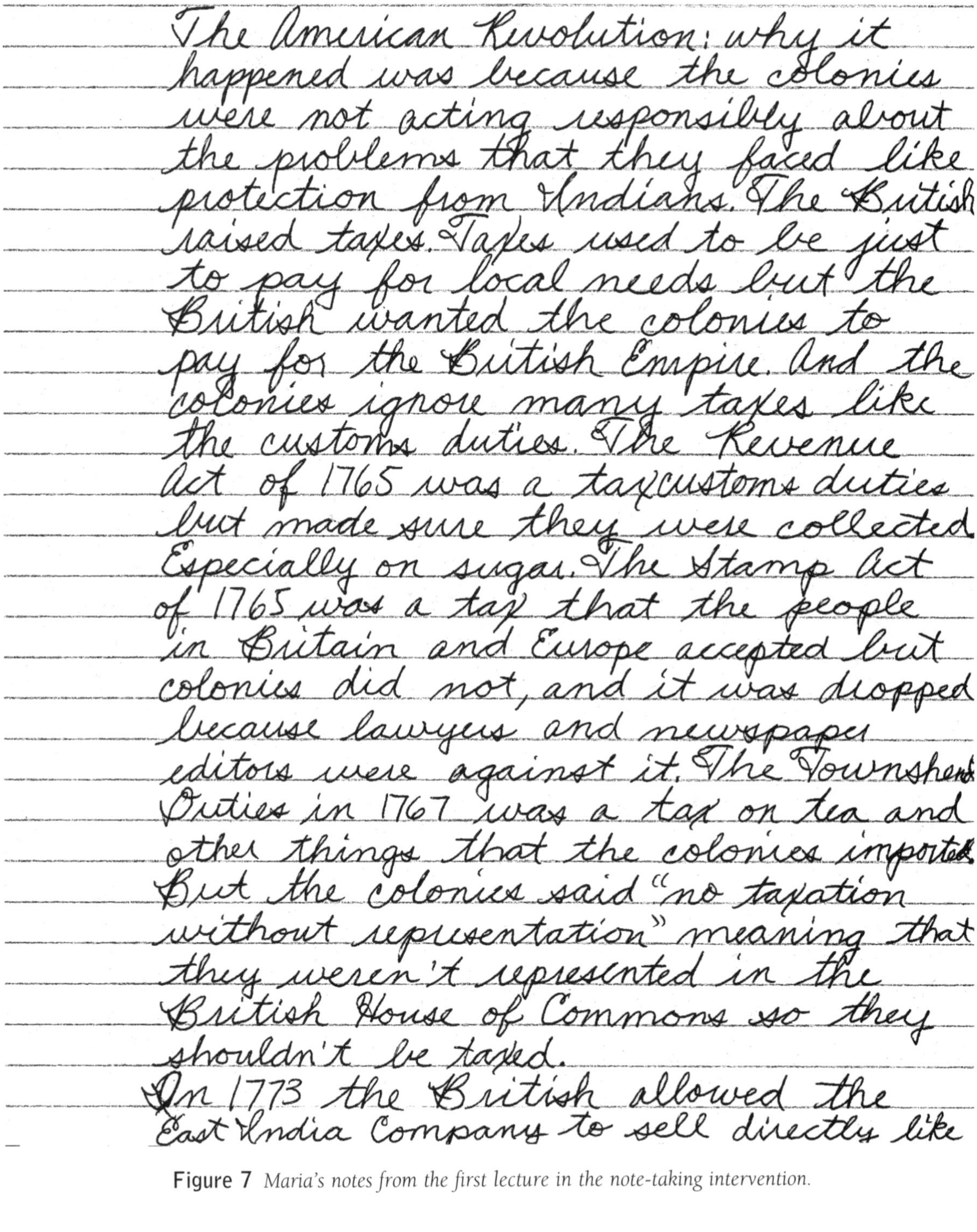

The American Revolution: why it happened was because the colonies were not acting responsibly about the problems that they faced like protection from Indians. The British raised taxes. Taxes used to be just to pay for local needs but the British wanted the colonies to pay for the British Empire. And the colonies ignore many taxes like the customs duties. The Revenue Act of 1765 was a taxcustoms duties but made sure they were collected Especially on sugar. The Stamp Act of 1765 was a tax that the people in Britain and Europe accepted but colonies did not, and it was dropped because lawyers and newspaper editors were against it. The Townshend Duties in 1767 was a tax on tea and other things that the colonies imported But the colonies said "no taxation without representation" meaning that they weren't represented in the British House of Commons so they shouldn't be taxed.
In 1773 the British allowed the East India Company to sell directly like

Figure 7 *Maria's notes from the first lecture in the note-taking intervention.*

to customers like the colonies instead of just at auctions in London. This means that colonial tea merchants would not have that business any more. So there were boycotts against tea in every colonial port and the Boston Tea Party was when colonials disguised as Indians invaded tea ships and dumped the tea into the harbor. Britain closed the port of Boston. This harbor was one of the most important economic thing in Mass. colony. And the British took back the charter of Mass. and stopped local elections and made it illegal to hold town meetings.

The Untolerable Acts were closing down Mass. and giving a new shape to Quebec that included Wisconsin, Mich. Illnois, Indiana and Ohio.

Then colonists sent delegates to the continental congress in Philadelphia.

Figure 7 *Continued.*

be carefully monitored to determine if it is working. With this in mind, we will discuss a number of strategies that might be considered.

1. Recording strategies. Be selective about what you include in your notes. Write down only main ideas and supporting facts. Listen for summary statements and write them down. Listen for signal words, for example, "there are four reasons." Trying to write everything down burdens a student with trivia and often results in the student's not being able to keep up with the lecture.

2. Linear outlines. A revision strategy involving a linear framework lists the topics and subtopics in traditional outline form, leaving room in between for note taking.

3. Mapping outlines. A revision strategy involving the use of graphic representations to relate information visually, such as tree diagrams, flow charts, concept webs, and two-dimensional matrices. The type of visual structure must be chosen on the basis of the material, for example, a lecture comparing and contrasting religions can be captured using a two dimensional matrix.

4. Cornell system. The written page is divided vertically with one column for recording and another for revising using one or more of the revision strategies listed above.

Choosing Appropriate Note-Taking Strategies

Calvin's and Maria's efforts illustrate how goals emerge from analyses of the specifics of note-taking procedures and how students can plan strategies to meet their note-taking goals.

> Now that note-taking was required and evaluated by his teacher, *Calvin* began to keep a social studies notebook. Because his self-monitoring revealed that his notes were meager and fragmentary, he decided

to adopt several recording strategies recommended by his teacher. He tried to select and write down only main ideas and supporting facts. Main ideas would be marked by an asterisk, and supporting ideas would be enumerated. He listened for summary statement cues and signal words, such as "in summary" or "there are five reasons" to guide his note-taking. He set as his goal the following averages: four main ideas, eight supportive facts, one list, and no revisions during each daily teaching session.

Maria saw that her history notes were not very detailed, and she attributed their superficiality to not knowing which comments of her teacher were most important. She decided to focus attention on the note-taking of a good student who sat next to her as a model for encoding key information. When the student made written entries, she would include the points being discussed in her own notes. Her goal was to increase her main ideas to eight, supporting facts to 24, lists to two, and not to bother with revisions.

STRATEGY IMPLEMENTATION AND MONITORING

Students should spend the second week of this self-regulatory exercise implementing the note-taking strategies that they have chosen. Because the pace of this self-regulatory exercise is not established by students themselves, the teacher may experience some pressure from the class to dwell longer on ideas or otherwise slow down the rate at which he or she conducts the class. It is helpful if the teacher provides outlines of the lesson plans for students to use to compare the completeness and organization of their notes at the end of each class. These outlines may be useful for students who, in an effort to improve their usual note-taking methods, may miss key material.

The teacher may notice some students observing one another more than usual. Students may look for cues from their peers to help them gauge the relative importance of the material being covered. For example, the sight of many class members recording a particular idea in their notes would signal its importance. Some students with exemplary note-taking skills may be regarded as models for the class, and their individual note-taking behavior could guide other students' efforts.

Let us return to our students.

> *Calvin's* meager note-taking goals hindered his progress in social studies. In his notes, he averaged three main ideas, six supporting facts, no lists, and no revisions. His note-taking grades improved slightly to 5 because of increases in note length, and his quiz scores remained at 5 because he didn't know how to use his notes to study. His self-efficacy increased slightly to 6, indicating some confidence that he could earn 6 on his quiz (i.e., $6 + 0 = 6$).
>
> *Maria's* decision to observe a higher achieving peer paid off to some degree. She captured five main ideas, 10 supporting facts, and one list, but she did not review or rewrite her notes. Her score on her notes went up to 6, indicating some improvement in content. Her self-efficacy rating increased to 6 reflecting confidence that she would earn a 6 (i.e., $6 + 0 = 6$), but her quiz score remained unchanged at 6.

STRATEGIC-OUTCOME MONITORING

For students to refine their methods, the teacher needs to provide opportunities for them to put their strategies to practice repeatedly. We recommend an additional 2 weeks for strategy refinement. During these weeks, the teacher looks for disparities between students' quiz scores and their self-efficacy ratings. At every opportunity, the teacher directs students' attention to specific features of their note-taking. Regardless of whether a student expresses excitement at improvements in the quality of note-taking and quiz performance or frustration at difficulties and grades, the teacher focuses on the strategic processes underlying the student's sentiment.

Peer assistance and teacher involvement are crucial ingredients to strategy refinement, as we can see in our two illustrative students.

> *Calvin* began his note-taking strategy, and the amount of information he recorded during class began to increase. In his second week of applying the strategy, he recorded an average of five main ideas and 10 supporting facts. There was one list but no revisions. His notes earned a score of 6, and his quiz grade went up 1 point to 6. When he saw the value of this strategy, his self-efficacy rating also improved to 7, indicating that he was quite sure about earning a 7 (i.e., $7 + 0 = 7$). From discussions with other students, Calvin decided that he needed to revise his notes into outline form to make them easier to study, and he set a goal of one revision. As he studied, he decided to put a question mark to indicate any area where he felt that the information was either confusing or missing. He would answer those questions by asking his friends, by reading the text, or by asking questions of the teacher on the following day.
>
> Calvin's question marks were truly enlightening. He found that he had recorded 20 supporting facts for the 10

	Week	Process/feedback/plan
Table 5		Calvin's Self-Regulated Development of Note-Taking Skills

	Week	Process/feedback/plan
Self-evaluation and monitoring	1	*Processes monitored*: Daily averages in social studies: main ideas = 1, supporting facts = 2, lists = 0, revisions = 0 *Feedback*: Notes scored = 3, quiz = 3, self-efficacy = 5
Planning and goal setting		*Goal*: Increase daily average of main ideas to 4, supporting facts to 8, lists to 1, but no revisions. *Strategy*: Mark the main ideas with asterisks and enumerate the supporting points
Strategy implementation and monitoring	2	*Processes monitored*: Daily averages: main ideas = 3, supporting facts = 6, lists = 0, revisions = 0 *Feedback*: Notes scored = 5, quiz = 5, self-efficacy = 6
Strategic-outcome monitoring	3	*Processes monitored*: Daily averages: main ideas = 5, supporting facts = 10, lists = 1, revisions = 0 *Feedback*: Notes scored = 6, quiz = 6, self-efficacy = 7 *New goal*: Increase revisions to 1 *New strategy*: Add "?" where he was confused in his revisions and follow up by reading text, asking friends, or asking teacher
	4	*Processes monitored*: Main ideas = 10, supporting facts = 20, lists = 2, revisions = 1 *Feedback*: Notes scores = 8, quiz = 8, self-efficacy = 8

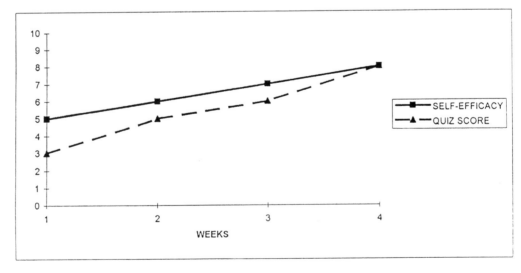

Figure 8 *Calvin's plotted outcome scores by week of note-taking intervention.*

main ideas and two lists and a revision. His notes and his quiz both earned him scores of 8, and his self-efficacy rating, at 8, indicated his absolute confidence in getting a 7 (i.e., $7 + 1 = 8$). (See Table 5 and Figure 8.)

As *Maria* continued to apply her strategy of attending to her classmate for a second week, she increased the number of main ideas captured in her notes to six and her supporting facts to 10. She averaged one list and no revisions. Her feedback remained the same, with a notes score of 4 and a quiz score of 6. Her self-efficacy remained the same at 6, indicating her awareness that she had not gained any more from this strategy. Therefore, she decided that she should also rewrite her notes. She would count each revision in her notes that resulted in a reorganization of the material as one revision, and she set a preliminary goal of one revision. Her strategy would be to rewrite her notes in outline form.

The following week, Maria made significant gains. She counted eight main ideas and 20 supporting facts, in addition to two lists. She also achieved her goal of a revision in her notes. Exhibit 8 shows the outline of the lecture that the teacher delivered. Figures 9 and 10 present Maria's class notes and her revision.

The score for her notes increased to 8; her quiz score increased to 7; and her self-efficacy rating rose to 7, indicating that she was quite certain of gaining a 7 on the quiz (i.e., $7 + 0 = 7$).

Table 6 shows the processes involved as Maria improved her note-taking skills.

EXHIBIT 8 **The Teacher's Outline of the Final Lecture in the Note-Taking Intervention.**

Civil War

   -part of the national consolidation and empire building that was occurring else-where in the 1860s (Japan, German, Austria, Hungary, Italy, Russian empire, Dominion of Canada).

1. Growth of the U.S.—territorial expansion (map) and rapid growth:

   -by 1860 31 million, more populous than G.B., almost as populous as France

   -pop. growth due to high birth rate and new immigrants, mostly from England, Ireland, and Germany

   Q. How does a large influx of immigrants affect the culture of the new host country? (Note that anti-foreign sentiments sometimes erupted but quickly subsided; contrast with current perceptions)

      -new traditions have to be incorporated (no effort to force immigrants to become "Americanized"—could maintain churches, newspapers, and social gatherings based on their home cultures)

      -language (English maintained as the dominant language, not a problem for English and Irish, and Germans readily learned)

      -new values need to be adopted by immigrants (they readily took to ideas of self-government, individual liberty, free enterprise, and unbounded opportunity for self-improvement)

      -summary: the American way impressed new immigrants, and established Americans became impressed with itself in the process—a new national identity was being consolidated.

2. Estrangement of North and South—at the same time the economic unity of the nation was falling apart.

A. -Industrial Revolution affected North and South differently

   -South became economically associated with G.B., chief supplier of raw cotton for British mills

   -cotton was a cash crop, South produced no manufactured goods, wanted to buy manufactured goods as cheap as possible, wanted free trade with G.B.

   -North built factories, owners and workers wanted protection from inflow of British goods (most competitive products in the world)

   Q. What would the North and the South's positions be related to tariffs? (North favor, South opposed)

B. -status of labor: the demand for cotton became enormous so the South fell deeply into the slavery and plantation system—the cheapest way to produce cotton (King Cotton)

Q. When you say a country has cheap labor, is that from the perspective of the person doing the work or the person buying the produce of that labor? (labor is never cheap from the standpoint of the laborer)

    -slavery is morally unacceptable around Europe, abolished

        in British colonies 1833

        in French colonies 1848

        in Latin America during the first half of 19th cent

        serfdom abolished in Hapsburg possessions in 1848

        serfdom abolished in Russia in 1861

-but American South increased importation of slaves

Q. It is usually clear how terrible slavery is to black people. How does the existence of a mass of subservient and unpaid laborers hurt white workers?

    -new immigrant laborers settled in the North; South remained Anglo-Saxon (no Irish, no German); in dense areas pop. was 50% African descent

3. Territorial expansion

    -South wanted to establish new plantations

    -North wanted to set up small farms, found new towns, build railroads, create markets

Q. As the Civil War approached, the North and South competed for control of new territories west of the Mississippi. What similar events had occurred prior to the Revolutionary War? (G.B. and France competing for the land west of the Alleghenies)

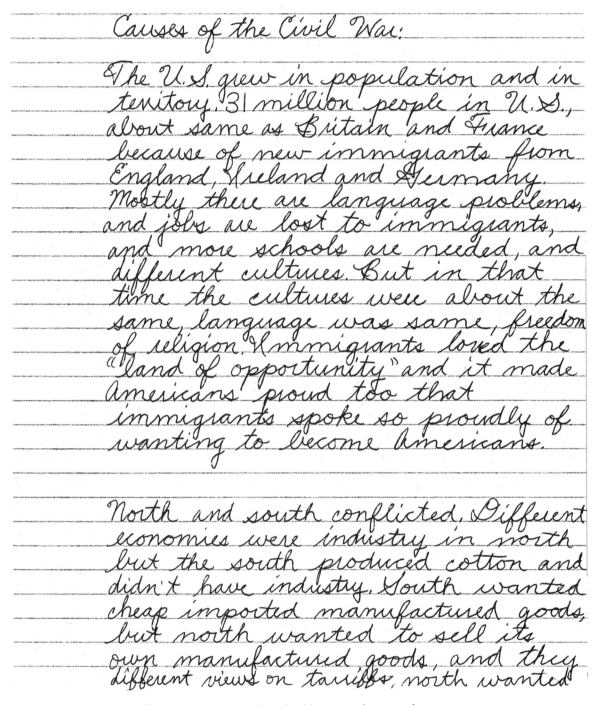

Causes of the Civil War:

The U.S. grew in population and in territory. 31 million people in U.S., about same as Britain and France because of new immigrants from England, Ireland and Germany. Mostly there are language problems, and jobs are lost to immigrants, and more schools are needed, and different cultures. But in that time the cultures were about the same, language was same, freedom of religion. Immigrants loved the "land of opportunity" and it made Americans proud too that immigrants spoke so proudly of wanting to become Americans.

North and south conflicted. Different economies were industry in north but the south produced cotton and didn't have industry. South wanted cheap imported manufactured goods, but north wanted to sell its own manufactured goods, and they different views on tariffs, north wanted

Figure 9 *Maria's class notes of the final lecture in the note-taking intervention.*

high tariffs and south wanted low. Immigrants who came in couldn't find work in south because slaves were cheap labor. Slavery was made illegal everywhere else in Britain, France, Latin America and Russia. But American imported more and more slaves. In the south sometimes 50% of the people were African-Americans.

West of the Mississippi there was "westward expansion". South wanted new plantations but north wanted railroads and towns. This was the same as before the R.R. when France and England fought for control of the west.

Figure 9 *Continued*

Causes of the Civil War:

The U.S. grew in population:

-31 million people (same as Britain and France)
-reason: immigrants from England, Ireland and Germany.

No problem with immigrants except they only worked in the north.

-language the same (English)
-no problem with their churches and social groups
-"American identity" was that immigrants were proud to become Americans and Americans were proud of that (land of opportunity).

Figure 10 *Maria's revised class notes of the final lecture in the note-taking intervention.*

Conflict between North and South:

South	North
cotton growing "King Cotton"	industry and manufacturing
wanted cheap imported manufactured goods	wanted to sell its own manufactured goods
wanted no tariffs on imported goods	wanted high tariffs on imported goods to protect their growing industry
no place for immigrants to work because slaves were cheap labor (not cheap from the slaves point of view)	immigrants worked there so the culture became rich and diverse
slaves increased in population to	blacks were free

Figure 10 *Continued.*

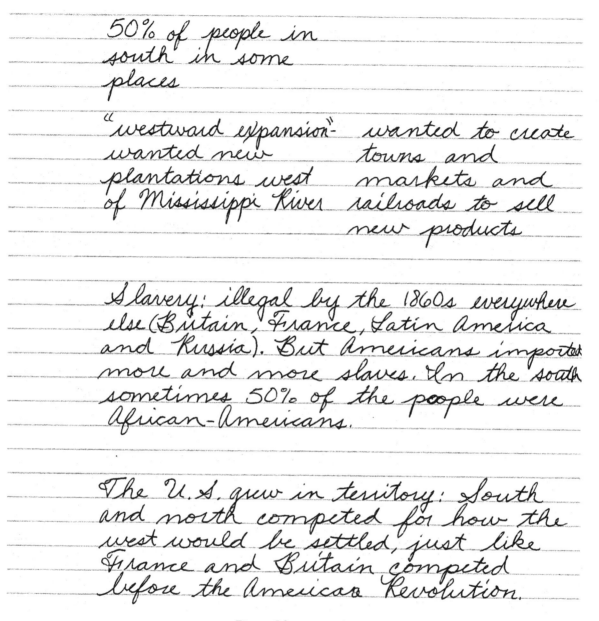

50% of people in
south in some
places

"westward expansion"-   wanted to create
wanted new   towns and
plantations west   markets and
of Mississippi River   railroads to sell
                        new products

Slavery: illegal by the 1860s everywhere
else (Britain, France, Latin America
and Russia). But Americans imported
more and more slaves. In the south
sometimes 50% of the people were
African-Americans.

The U.S. grew in territory: South
and north competed for how the
west would be settled, just like
France and Britain competed
before the American Revolution.

Figure 10 *Continued.*

	Week	Process/feedback/plan
Table 6		Maria' Self-Regulated Development of Note-Taking Skills

	Week	Process/feedback/plan
Self-evaluation and monitoring	1	*Processes monitored*: Daily averages in history: main ideas = 3, supporting facts = 7, lists = 1, revisions = 0 *Feedback*: Notes scored = 5, quiz = 6, self-efficacy = 5
Planning and goal setting		*Goal*: Increase daily average of main ideas to 8, supporting facts to 24, lists to 2, no revisions *Strategy*: Observe when high-achieving students take notes and follow suit
Strategy implementation and monitoring	2	*Processes monitored*: Daily averages: main ideas = 5, supporting facts = 10, lists = 1, revisions = 0 *Feedback*: Notes scored = 6, quiz = 6, self-efficacy = 6
Strategic-outcome monitoring	3	*Processes monitored*: Daily averages: main ideas = 6, supporting facts = 10, lists = 1, revisions = 0 *Feedback*: Notes scores = 6, quiz = 6, self-efficacy = 6 *New goal*: Revise notes once *New strategy*: Rewrite notes in outline form
	4	*Processes monitored*: Daily averages: main ideas = 8, supporting facts = 20, lists = 2, revision = 1 *Feedback*: Notes scored = 8, quiz = 7, self-efficacy = 7

SELF-EFFICACY PERCEPTIONS

The development and effective use of class notes are essential for academic learning because teachers not only convey important information orally but also signal how the students should evaluate information from text sources. When note-taking achieves this additional goal, students will experience an enhanced sense of self-efficacy to perform on exams. Self-efficacy growth should accompany evidence from the students' monitoring sheets of improved note-taking.

> Effective note-taking goes well beyond accurate recording to include revisions that make the material increasingly meaningful to the student.

EXHIBIT 9 | **Teacher's Checklist for Developing Students' Note-Taking Skills**

1. Planning
   ___ Plan note-taking activities (see implementation, below) lasting 5 weeks in such a way that they mesh well with the curriculum
   ___ Make sure that note-taking assignments are equal in length and difficulty

2. Implementation
   Week 1
   ___ Review concept of self-efficacy and how to calculate it
   ___ Prepare and administer 10-question quizzes at end of each week (for testing note-taking skills and as basis for students' self-efficacy judgments)
   ___ Prepare adequate supply of a note-taking chart similar to that shown in Exhibit 7
   ___ Explain how to record data on the note-taking chart
   Week 2–4
   ___ Model goal setting and strategy selection in early weeks
   ___ Demonstrate how to graph self-efficacy and quiz scores and self-efficacy and process goal attainments
   ___ Keep records of students' self-efficacy and quiz scores
   ___ Review students' graphed data after 2–3 weeks (i.e., self-efficacy and quiz scores or self-efficacy and process goal attainments)
   ___ Determine whether there is congruence between self-efficacy and quiz scores for each student. If not, data may indicate the need for teacher's attention to "stand out" students (either overly high or low in perceived self-efficacy, given quiz results)

3. Follow-up
   ___ Plan and implement note-taking follow up activities for some time later in the course (to reinforce prior time management learning and to generalize this learning to other assignments or tasks)

The teacher can increase students' awareness of these corresponding changes by asking them to graph their self-efficacy ratings along with the measures of note-taking. For example, the teacher can guide students to produce line graphs, with their ratings for self-efficacy and the measures of their process goals across time. These graphs can motivate students to maintain their strategic efforts to improve their note taking. As students develop a sense of the connection among their strategic efforts, their feelings of con-

1 In what aspects of note taking will your students' need the most of help?

2 Which aspects of the Note-Taking Self-Monitoring Form will be most helpful for your students? Are there any aspects of the form you might you wish to change? If so, describe how they could be adapted.

3 What problems do you anticipate in helping your students to self-monitor their note taking?

4 Describe the note-taking strategies that will be most helpful to your students, and explain why the strategies could help.

fidence, and improvements in their graded performance, they should develop regular habits of maintaining notes that are complete, organized, and coherent.

To assist you in implementing this self-regulatory cycle for students' note taking, we have provided a checklist in Exhibit 9.

SELECTED READINGS

Kierwa, K. A. (1989). A review of note-taking: The encoding-storage paradigm and beyond. *Educational Psychology Review*, *1*, 147–172.

King, A. (1992). Comparison of self-questioning, summarizing, and note-taking-review as strategies for learning from lectures. *American Educational Research Journal*, *29*, 303–323.

King, A. (1995). Cognitive strategies for learning from direct teaching. Reading comprehension strategies. In E. Wood, V. E. Woloshyn, & T. Willoughby (Eds.), *Cognitive strategy instruction for middle and high schools* (pp. 18–65). Cambridge, MA: Bookline Books.

goal 5

Developing Test Anticipation
and Preparation Skills

Unfortunately, students, parents, and teachers often hold test scores as the holy grail of intellectual accomplishment. They are not. It is possible for students to know material and not do well on exams. Although students may know answers to many of the items not tested, they may do less well on those appearing on an exam. In addition, extraneous variables, such as distractions, external pressures, or students' psychological states, may impede test performance. Nevertheless, it is true that students who are well prepared for an exam are more likely to do well than those who have not prepared adequately.

Like the three most important considerations when purchasing real estate, "location, location, location," adequate exam preparation boils down to three words: "review, review, review." Essentially, a proper test review involves three phases: (a) regular, weekly reviews that consolidate short-term learning; (b) systematic reviews prior to exams, and (c) postexam reviews, or learning from one's exam performance. It is important to emphasize that the second phase is not equivalent to cramming. Cramming is the antithesis of high-quality review because it leads, at best, to short-term learning and quite often to frustration and anxiety. The systematic, low-stress review we advocate here produces long-term, integrated intellectual growth.

> Correct exam preparation is built on efficient time management, skillful text summarization, and high-quality note-taking and review.

Test anticipation and preparation skills are interrelated with and mutually reinforcing of the three skills we have presented so far. We recommend that teachers engage in this exercise after students have adjusted to the cyclic nature of self-regulatory skill development.

A problem in learning how to prepare for exams is the time lag between them, which is too long to enable students to make corrective efforts while the feedback is still fresh in their mind. Quizzes are not appropriate vehicles for developing test-taking skills because they tend to cover only limited amounts of material. To provide students the best opportunity to develop their test anticipation and preparation skills, we suggest that teachers prepare short proto-exams that provide shorter time lags than real exams while covering more material. Proto-exams should include samples of each of the item types usually found on a regular exam. To save administration time, teachers may ask students to answer essay questions in outline form.

This exercise can be carried out over a period of the school year during which two or three exams would regularly be administered. The teacher needs to develop approximately six proto-exams of consistent scope, difficulty level, and blend of question format. The teacher encourages students to maintain a daily record of efforts they make to anticipate upcoming exams, to review their strategic efforts during weekly class sessions, and to gain feedback from their performance on proto-exams.

SELF-EVALUATION AND MONITORING

The teacher can introduce this self-regulatory exercise by asking students to rate their self-efficacy for having prepared thoroughly enough to do well on a forthcoming exam and by using the rating method similar to that used in prior exercises, which we will explain below. Following the administration of the exam, the teacher can use the results to guide students in analyzing their missed items. Students can be given a simple form such as the one in Exhibit 10 for monitoring these features, and they can classify the missed items on the previous exam. Students can record that information and their self-efficacy ratings on the monitoring sheets and indicate how much time they prepared for the exam. The next phase of this self-regulatory exercise will not begin until approximately one-third of the time toward the next exam has passed. For example, a teacher who administers a major exam every three months would introduce the next phase of the cycle one month after initial evaluation and self-monitoring. Therefore, the teacher asks students to retain their self-monitoring sheets for the future.

The teacher can present self-efficacy assessment using the question, "How sure do I feel that I am reviewing thoroughly enough to do well on the upcoming exam?" Assuming that the proto-exam can be scored on a 0 to 100 scale like regular examinations, self-efficacy is defined as the estimated score on the proto-exam after a 10-point adjustment on the basis of the students' confidence in their answer. The teacher asks the students to estimate the score they expect to receive on the quiz and then to rate their confidence about attaining at least that score using a 3-

Date of Exam	Review		Analysis of Missed Items			Self-Efficacy
	Weekly	Immediate	In Notes	Not in Notes	Question Type	

category scale (representing *not very sure, quite sure,* and *absolutely sure*). To adjust the estimated score for differences in confidence, the following weighting procedure should be used. For the rating of not very sure, 10 points are subtracted from the estimated score (-10); for the rating of quite sure, no points are added or subtracted from the estimated score (0); for the rating of absolutely sure, 10 points are added to the estimated score ($+10$). Essentially, this system is a variant of the earlier self-efficacy rating system that is expanded by a factor of ten in both the grade estimation and confidence adjustment (i.e., from 0–10 to 0–100).

Three very important pieces of information can be gathered from the self-monitoring form. First, students can check missed items against their notes to see whether their note-taking skills were adequate to capture information pertinent to missed items. If notes do not contain information that was tested, upgrading of note-taking skills is indicated. Second, if information was captured in the notes but questions were missed on that material, the students' review methods are suspect. Third, if students' error patterns relate to question type, test-anticipation methods are suspect. Students can also record how thoroughly they review by maintaining time records regarding these sessions.

Let us examine the specific information teachers may encounter by reviewing Calvin's record.

> Because of *Calvin's* improvement in math due to his time-management strategy, he applied the strategy to his homework assignments in Spanish as well. He began this homework when he returned home after school instead of waiting until the evening, and he improved his homework and quiz scores in Spanish. As a result of his increased homework time, he raised his course average from barely passing to C+, but he was still not earning the B average he wanted on his report card, largely because his exam scores were mediocre. When it came to exams, his strategy for success was to "psych out the teacher" or

try to figure out what the teacher might do to "trick" students on the test. Unfortunately, in Calvin's case it seemed that it was he himself who became fooled by the exams. He put in no time for regular review and resorted to last-minute cramming during the evening before the exam. The missed items were mostly in his notes, and they usually involved vocabulary items. Right before the previous Spanish exam, he had rated his self-efficacy at 60, indicating he was quite confident that he would earn at least a 60 (i.e., $60 + 0 = 60$), which is exactly what he earned.

GOAL SETTING AND STRATEGIC PLANNING

A few weeks following the previous exam, the teacher asked students in Calvin's class to begin planning on how they will prepare for the proto-exam. The teacher advised students to bring to class their monitoring sheets from which they will set their strategic-process goals. The planning and goal setting phase is complex for this self-regulation exercise because proper preparation requires many interrelated elements. Students' strategies will necessarily include time planning and management as well as specific review methods. The teacher encourages students to keep their strategies simple because they typically have difficulty modifying several aspects of their study methods simultaneously. In addition to these problems of strategy implementation, students must deal with varying outcome feedback, which can be difficult to interpret, and this can impair further strategy refinement.

Selected Test-Preparation Strategies

Listed below are some commonly used strategies to prepare for tests. The list illustrates strategies that have been effective. In addition, students may wish to refer to other sources for additional strategies (see *Selected Readings*) or to develop their own strategies. Each strategy should be chosen only when it is appropriate, and it should be carefully monitored to determine if it is working. With this in mind, we will discuss a number of strategies that might be considered.

1. Revising lecture and text notes. Trying to memorize all oral and textual matter is a recipe for failure. Instead, students should concentrate on organizing only the most important information using one of the revision strategies.

2. Elaborative interrogation. Students ask themselves questions intended to produce elaborations of the test material (e.g., Why is each fact true?). This strategy helps integrate new material with information already known.

3. Representational imagery. Lists of new words or concepts can be recalled by forming a vivid image of the word and its definition (e.g., the Spanish word *pan* can be associated with its meaning *bread* by creating an image of bread in a metal pan).

4. First-letter mnemonics. This strategy entails remembering the first letter for each of a list of key words. For example, the names for the Great Lakes could be encoded in the form of the word *HOMES* (Huron, Ontario, Michigan, Erie, and Superior). Another example is the word *FACE* to describe the spaces on the treble clef of the music staff.

5. Mnemonic sentences. A variant on the previous strategy, wherein students remember a series of facts by constructing a sentence starting with the same letters, for example, "my very eccentric mother just served us nine pizzas." The initial letters of the words in this sentence are the same as for the planets in the solar system, starting nearest the sun—Mercury, Venus, Earth, Mars, Jupiter, Saturn, Uranus, Neptune, and Pluto.

6. Use of study partner. This strategy involves finding a classmate to compare study notes and to mutually test each other to self-evaluate one's test preparation.

Choosing Appropriate Test-Preparation Strategies

Let us consider how Calvin analyzed the task and set an appropriate process goal and strategy.

> Although *Calvin* did his Spanish homework regularly, he did not review on a regular basis. He interpreted his initial self-evaluation results to mean that he should improve the way he reviewed for his Spanish test. If he put aside some time each week to review his class and homework notes, he would simultaneously increase his review time and would focus specifically on the area that seemed to need the most improvement. His goal was to reduce the number of vocabulary items he missed that were in his notes, and his strategy was to reorganize his notes by rewriting them to identify and organize vocabulary items.

STRATEGY IMPLEMENTATION AND MONITORING

It is important that students get feedback on how well their strategies are working as they begin to implement them.

Because exams are infrequently administered, the feedback cycle is long, and this deters strategy refinement. We have developed the notion of proto-exams to provide a more proximal type of feedback. In the ensuing weeks, the teacher can administer proto-exams (whose results need not be considered in determining the students' course grades). The proto-exams serve to break the material into discrete units. The teacher should introduce the first of these proto-exams two weeks after the students have established their strategic plans.

> *Calvin* had put in a couple of hours each week to rewrite his Spanish notes to identify and organize vocabulary items, and he

put in his normal preparation time on the night before the proto-exam. Nevertheless, he still missed 12 vocabulary items that had been in his notes. He scored a 65 on the proto-exam, and his self-efficacy rose slightly to 63, indicating that he was quite sure of attaining a 63 (i.e., $63 + 0 = 63$).

STRATEGIC-OUTCOME MONITORING

By offering proto-exams every 2 weeks, teachers can provide students with repeated opportunities to refine their strategies. Proto-exams are most effective if they closely resemble the types of items of actual exams but cover less material and are briefer in length. Let us see how Calvin prepared for a proto-exam.

Calvin continued to rewrite his Spanish notes as preparation for the next proto-exam. He tried to be more careful, putting more time than he had the first time he applied the vocabulary-organization strategy. The benefits he had to show for this effort were a continued reduction in the number of items he missed, but he still missed 10 items that were in his notes. His proto-exam score increased again to 70, as did his self-efficacy rating, indicating that he was quite certain of earning a 70 (i.e., $70 + 0 = 70$). These moderate improvements in his achievement in Spanish made him think that revising his notes may not be enough and that he ought to also find ways to commit those vocabulary words to memory. He decided to try to apply some powerful mnemonic strategies to key terms in the outlines, possibly by forming images of the concepts (elaborative rehearsal) or by creating verbal acronyms. His revised notes were fairly

	Preparation Period	Process/feedback/plan
Table 7		**Calvin's Self-Regulated Development of Test Anticipation and Preparation Skills**
Self-evaluation and monitoring	1	*Processes monitored*: Spanish weekly review = none, immediate review = 1 hour, missed items in notes = 15, missed items not in notes = 2, missed question types = vocabulary items *Feedback*: Exam score = 60 (out of 100), self-efficacy = 60
Planning and goal setting		*Goal*: Reduce missed items in notes *Strategy*: Start weekly review to identify and reorganize vocabulary items in notes
Strategy implementation and monitoring	2	*Processes monitored*: Weekly review = 2 hours, immediate review = 1 hour, missed items in notes = 12, missed items not in notes = 0, missed question types = vocabulary items *Feedback*: Proto-exam score = 65, self-efficacy = 63
Strategic-outcome monitoring	3	*Processes monitored*: Weekly review = 3 hours, immediate review = 1 hour, missed items in notes = 10, missed items not in notes = 0, missed question types = vocabulary items *Feedback*: Proto-examine score = 70, self-efficacy = 70 *New strategy*: Apply mnemonic aids to outlined notes
	4	*Processes monitored*: Weekly review = 4 hours, immediate review = 45 minutes, missed items in notes = 3, missed items not in notes = 0, missed question types = vocabulary items *Feedback*: Proto-exam score = 85, self-efficacy = 90

concise, and he now would spend time memorizing the words using representational imagery that connect words, such as the Spanish word *derecho* (right) with an image of his right hand. As Calvin formed images and verbal acronyms, he was able to integrate the new information with his existing knowledge.

Calvin increased his regular weekly review because of the demands of his representational strategy. Interestingly, he found that this strategy reduced the time he needed for review immediately prior to the proto-exam to just 45 minutes. The test benefits were also evident: His proto-exam score improved to 85. During the course of this self-regulatory exercise, Calvin reduced his missing items from 17 to 3 through specific procedures he applied following analyses of his process-monitoring forms. His self-efficacy rose to 90, indicating that he was very sure of attaining that grade (i.e., 80 + 10 = 90). His confidence stemmed from his awareness of the effectiveness of not only his exam anticipation and preparation skills but also his self-regulatory skill improvement.

Table 7 shows the processes involved as Calvin improved his test anticipation and preparation skills.

SELF-EFFICACY PERCEPTIONS

Calvin's self-efficacy perceptions regarding test outcomes depended on his mnemonic-skill development. His outcome goals were improved grades on exams or proto-exams, but his self-efficacy perceptions were based on the strategic processes he used to achieve those goals. Because of their initial focus on strategically controllable processes, self-efficacy assessments—even when applied to as emo-

> Perceptions of self-efficacy are negatively correlated with anxiety. Students' increases in self-efficacy across homework assessments diminish the anxiety that often accompanies testing.

tional an issue as test preparation—should not be debilitating to even test-anxious students.

To assist you in implementing this self-regulatory cycle for students' test anticipation and preparation, we have provided a checklist in Exhibit 11.

EXHIBIT 11 | Teacher's Checklist for Developing Students' Test Anticipation and Preparation Skills

1. Planning
   ___ Plan test anticipation and preparation activities (See Implementation, below) over several units of study so that they mesh coherently with the curriculum
   ___ Make sure that test anticipation and preparation assignments are equal in length and difficulty

2. Implementation
   ___ Introduce concept of self-efficacy and how to calculate it
   ___ Introduce concept of proto-exam using item types and difficulty usually found on regular exams
   ___ Prepare adequate supply of a test anticipation and preparation chart similar to that shown in Exhibit 10
   ___ Model use of the test anticipation and preparation chart
   ___ Prepare and administer proto-exams every 2–3 weeks to provide adequate feedback to students on the effectiveness of their strategy use
   ___ Keep records of students' self-efficacy and proto-exam scores
   ___ Determine whether there is congruence between self-efficacy and proto-exam scores for each student. If not, data may indicate the need for teacher's attention to "stand out" students (either overly high or low in perceived self-efficacy, given proto-exam results)

3. Follow-up
   ___ Plan and implement time management follow up activities for some time later in the course (to reinforce prior exam anticipation and preparation skills)

1 In which aspects of test anticipation and preparation will your students need the most help?

2 Which sections of the Test Anticipation and Preparation Self-Monitoring Form will be most helpful for your students? Are there any sections of the form you might you wish to change, and if so, how could they be adapted?

3 What problems do you anticipate in helping your students self-monitor their test anticipation and preparation?

4 Describe the test anticipation and preparation strategies that will be most helpful to your students, and explain why the strategies could help.

SUGGESTED READINGS

Levin, J. R. (1993). Mnemonic strategies and classroom learning: A twenty-year report. *The Elementary School Journal*, *94*, 235–244.

Pressley, M., & Woloshyn, V. (1995). Learning facts: The value of always asking yourself why and other mnemonic strategies. In M. Pressley, V. Woloshyn, J. Burkell, T. Cariglia-Bull, L. Lysynchuk, J.A. McGoldrick, B. Schneider, B.L. Snyder, & S. Symons (Eds.), *Cognitive strategy instruction that really improves children's academic performance* (2nd ed. pp. 234–243). Cambridge, MA: Brookline Books.

Wood, E., & Willoughby, T. (1995). Cognitive strategies for test-taking. In E. Wood, V. E. Woloshyn, & T. Willoughby (Eds.), *Cognitive strategy instruction for middle and high schools* (pp. 245–258). Cambridge, MA: Brookline Books.

goal 6

Developing
Writing Skills

Although writing was traditionally taught during English and Language Arts classes, it is currently being taught and applied throughout the curriculum. Teachers tap their students' writing skills when they assign short-answer items for homework, include short-answer or essay items on tests, or require students to produce research reports. Teachers sometimes face overt classroom resistance to written assignments, and this opposition may actually dissuade some of them from assigning written projects. Using the following self-regulatory exercise, a teacher can offer students techniques to develop their writing skills, which may deflect resistance to writing assignments.

Adapting a self-regulatory approach to developing student writing skills offers benefits to teachers and students alike. Teachers who incorporate writing into their instruction extend students excellent opportunities to explore course material in terms of the organization of concepts and the critical examination of ideas. Not only do students who are given the opportunity to evaluate and critique one another's drafts get to explore one another's conceptual understanding of the topic, but their writing also improves because they discover the importance of good organization and clear statements. They understand the frustrations that readers face when reading grammatically flawed or misspelled pieces, and they may appreciate the meaning behind the critiques they receive of their own writing. Teachers can reap large benefits in terms of student participation, depth of content coverage, and the satisfaction of having contributed to the development of their students' literacy skills.

The self-regulatory approach again involves a series of assignments geared to help students focus on the specific processes of writing. The teacher assigns five reports over 5 weeks. The reports should be short enough to be written in 1 week (3–5 pages, more or less depending on the class), and they should be based on the course content currently covered. The teacher may allow students to choose which expository format they will use for presenting their ideas (e.g., comparison and contrast, problem and solution, explanation).

The teacher should prepare various stages of a model report, including raw notes, categorized notes, the beginning draft of text, revisions of clarity, and revisions for interest. The teacher should also provide students with the criteria for judging the reports' content, organization, clarity, and interest. Students score one another's reports according to the teacher's criteria. The teacher may consider assigning topics that integrate several days of homework. Thus, this self-regulatory exercise can be carried out in the time normally allocated to homework review.

SELF-EVALUATION AND MONITORING

The writing processes that we suggest for self-monitoring cover the basic activities necessary for developing ideas and for generating and revising text. After assigning the topic, the teacher guides students to self-monitor their writing processes each day using a simple form such as the one in Exhibit 12. By focusing on six benchmark activities, students can identify the aspects of their writing that lead to favorable comments and grades.

The teacher asks the students to start their writing by making notes of their ideas, categorizing the notes, turning those categories into units of text (e.g., a paragraph), and finally making changes to improve their text. The teacher models the processes involved in creating a report during the first week. We recommend that for tabulation purposes, a *note* can be considered an idea or thought, and it can be in the form of a phrase, a few words, or a sentence. Similarly, a change can be tabulated when the student rewrites a sentence or moves a sentence to a different

| Exhibit 12 | Writing Self-Monitoring Form | | | | |

Assigned Report # _____	Mon	Tue	Wed	Thur
How much time did I spend on the assigned report?				
How many notes did I make of what I want to say?				
How many notes did I organize within categories?				
How many categories did I turn into text?				
How many changes did I make to my report to improve its clarity?				
Self-efficacy?				

location. Students can adapt these general principles in their own way because consistency within the student's counting method is more important than consistency across students.

To make a self-efficacy rating, we will assume a 10-point scoring system for the reports with 2 points scored for satisfactorily meeting the content, organization, clarity, and interest criteria and 2 points for handing in the report on time. The teacher asks the students to estimate the score they expect to receive on the writing assignment and then to rate their confidence about attaining at least that score using a 3-point scale (representing "not very sure," "quite sure," and "absolutely sure"). To adjust the estimated score for differences in confidence, the following weighting procedure should be used. For the rating of "not very sure," a point is subtracted from the estimated score (-1); for the rating of "quite sure," no points are added or subtracted from the estimated score (0); and for the rating of "absolutely sure," a point is added to the estimated score ($+1$). Self-efficacy is defined as the estimated score after the point adjustment.

During the first week, the teacher invests a class session to model the writing process and the way a student would monitor his or her efforts. At the end of the week, the teacher has students exchange their reports and evaluate one another's work on the basis of criteria the teacher establishes. This criteria should specify content (main ideas and supporting ideas), organization (introduction, logical development with no misplaced ideas, and conclusion), clarity (grammar, choice of words, and sentence length), and interest (approach to the topic and use of examples). The teacher should ask students to note their average self-efficacy ratings on their papers and should collect them to record the scores. In the beginning of this exercise, the teacher may want to review peers' scoring to see how well it conforms to the established criteria and may want to note whether students' self-efficacy ratings are in accord with their performance.

Let us look at what Calvin and Maria learned from their self-monitoring and their peers' feedback on their first book report.

Calvin felt that he had never really learned the mechanics of writing. His book report, barely meeting the minimum length requirement, consisted of a single paragraph containing many incomplete and run-on sentences. Calvin's monitoring sheet showed that he had not started working on the report until Thursday night, when he spent 1 hour on it. He was not able to count either notes or revisions because he wrote the paper in a single draft directly from his thoughts. Figure 11 shows the first page of Calvin's report on *Treasure Island* (Stevenson, 1986). He earned a 3, indicating that he had handed it in on time and that it showed some understanding of the story content. Calvin rated his self-efficacy at 4, indicating that he was unsure of getting much more than a 4 on the report because of his poor writing skills (i.e., $4 - 0 = 4$).

Maria usually earned Bs in writing. She had a good vocabulary and could construct complete sentences. Her teachers had often commented that her ideas needed to be organized better, but Maria never understood what that meant. She thought that clarity at a sentence level was the most important aspect of writing. For example, although she was able to record that she worked on the book report every day for 30 minutes for 4 days, she didn't make many notes (only three) or develop them into categories (0) to generate text from them (0). Instead, she started working on the report by creating complete paragraphs from her few notes. On Thursday she recorded that she made 5 revisions or changes to improve the clarity that involved rewriting sentences. She had rated her self-efficacy at 9 because she felt quite

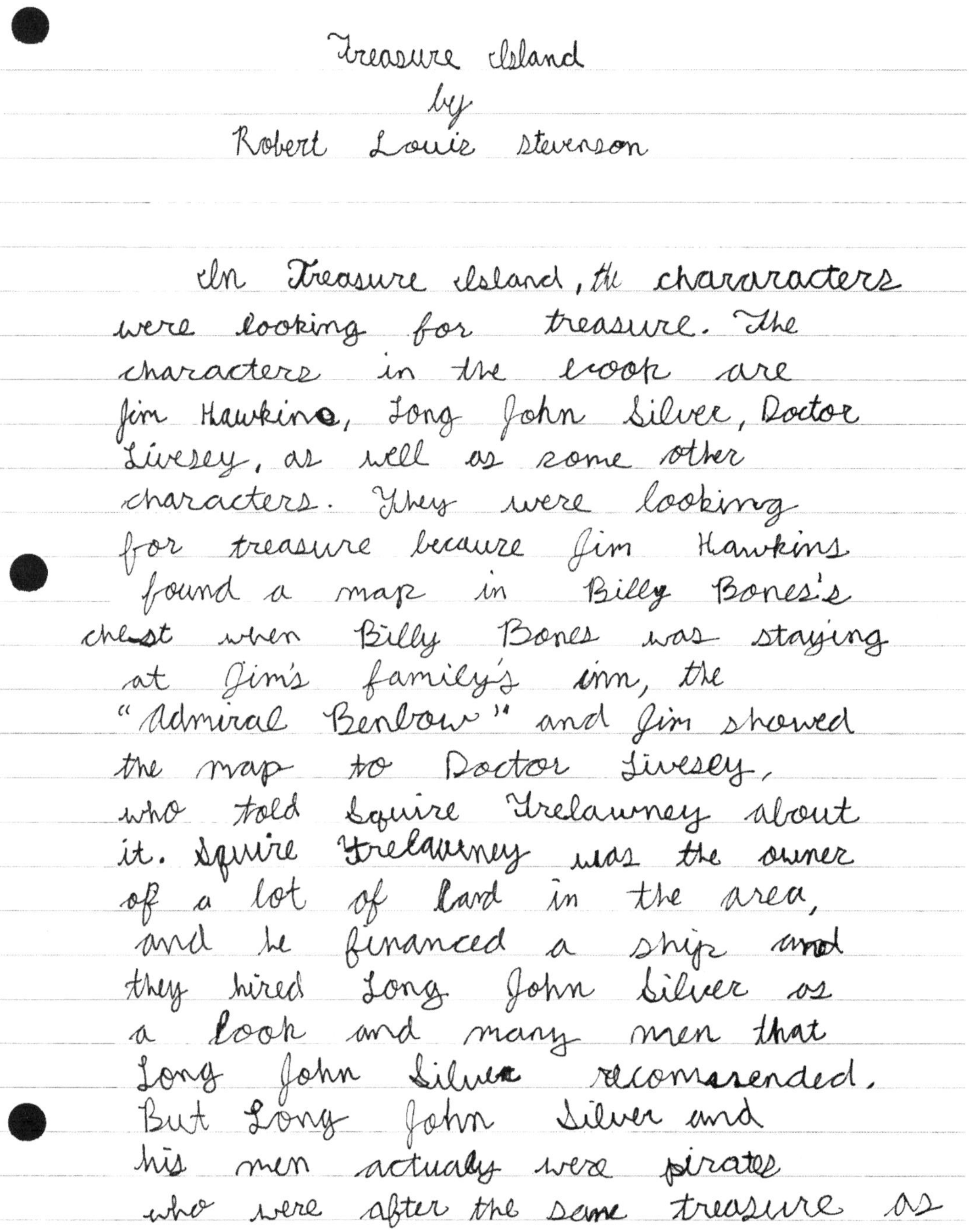

Treasure Island
by
Robert Louis Stevenson

In Treasure Island, the chararacters were looking for treasure. The characters in the book are Jim Hawkins, Long John Silver, Doctor Livesey, as well as some other characters. They were looking for treasure because Jim Hawkins found a map in Billy Bones's chest when Billy Bones was staying at Jim's family's inn, the "Admiral Benbow" and Jim showed the map to Doctor Livesey, who told Squire Trelawney about it. Squire Trelawney was the owner of a lot of land in the area, and he financed a ship and they hired Long John Silver as a cook and many men that Long John Silver recommended. But Long John Silver and his men actually were pirates who were after the same treasure as

Figure 11 *The first page of Calvin's first book report.*

sure of attaining at least a 9 (i.e., $9 + 0 = 9$). It turned out that this rating was an inflated perception of her skill. She scored a 6 because her book report was not well-organized, and she did not discuss the author's ideas in any depth.

GOAL SETTING AND STRATEGIC PLANNING

In the second week, the teacher asks students to set process goals for their strategic efforts to correct problem areas in their writing. These strategies focus students' attention on the activities necessary to produce good writing such as making notes, organizing notes, generating text, critiquing and revising, and seeking editorial assistance. The teacher highlights this process by asking students to reflect on the relationship among their writing activities, self-efficacy judgments, and external feedback. The teacher emphasizes the necessity (a) of each monitored activity and (b) of increasing the frequency of steps they neglected.

Selected Writing Strategies

Below are listed some strategies commonly used to write formal papers. The list illustrates several strategies that have been effective for the three main processes involved in writing: planning, drafting, and revising. In addition, students may wish to refer to other sources for additional strategies (see *Selected Readings* below) or to develop their own strategies. Each strategy should be chosen only when it is appropriate, and it should be carefully monitored to determine if it is working. With this in mind, we will discuss a number of strategies that might be considered.

1. Goal setting. The planning strategy for deciding the goals of the paper (e.g., to compare, to analyze, and to describe) and the subgoals (e.g., what things to compare, analyze, and describe).

2. Idea-generating questions. The drafting strategy of using questions to generate prose (e.g., what the object is, what the sequence of events is, what the facts on the object are, what the arguments or opinions are, and who the key players are).

3. Mapping or webbing. Planning strategies for establishing relations between ideas or events with visual concept maps or webs (e.g., linking scientists to key inventions, findings, and theories).

4. Varying sentence structure. The drafting strategy of trying to make sure paragraphs vary in structure from simple to compound and complex.

5. Imitating the experts. The drafting strategy of finding the work of a model writer and attempting to imitate the author's style of writing by rewriting a paper from memory.

6. Locating a peer editor. The revision strategy of finding an appropriate classmate to read and give feedback about various aspects of the draft.

7. Becoming a self-editor. The revision strategy of self-examining the draft by using a series of questions (e.g., Is there an introduction and conclusion? Did I achieve my main goal or was something omitted? Are any parts unclear or unsupported? Is the paper interesting? Did I give examples to illustrate important points?).

Choosing Appropriate Writing Strategies

Our two students illustrate how process goals establish clear mechanisms for students to begin developing their writing skills.

> *Calvin* seemed to lack the most basic writing skills, so he asked a classmate who was a good writer to help him. His partner suggested that he go over each sentence in his book report to make sure it was complete

(i.e., has a subject and verb) and bring some organization to the report by simply dividing it into paragraphs. Calvin set a goal to make sure each sentence was grammatical and to divide the draft of the report into at least three paragraphs. His strategy was to write a draft earlier in the week so that he would have time to revise it. His partner offered to give feedback on how well the book report was divided into different parts.

Maria did not understand why she had not earned at least an 8 on her previous book report. She knew that each of her sentences was clear. Her teacher noticed that her self-efficacy score was out of synch with the score on her report and offered her a suggestion. The teacher advised her that because her report seemed to lack depth, she might analyze each paragraph to determine its primary purpose and to count how many supporting ideas it contained. Partly to prove her teacher wrong, Maria did this. To her chagrin, she saw that the purpose or theme of many paragraphs was often restated in different forms, but it was not supported with facts or ideas. Maria set as process goals to combine categories of notes so that each paragraph contained at least three supporting facts. Her classroom partner offered to provide feedback on how well each paragraph would explain or illustrate an idea to someone who did not know much about the book.

STRATEGY IMPLEMENTATION AND MONITORING

As students begin to change their writing processes, it is important for them to monitor exactly what it is they are doing. This will help them in two ways: First, monitoring will tend to detect lapses back into old processes, and second, the students will be able to judge whether strategies seem to be leading to the improvements. As well as monitoring their strategic efforts, students should also continue to monitor how confident they feel about producing a well-written report. Students can be expected to feel an increasing sense of self-efficacy for writing during the course of this self-regulatory exercise.

> By having students attend to increasing feelings of self-efficacy, teachers will help instill in them a strategic orientation to skill development.

An additional benefit of self-regulatory instructional methods should be pointed out. Process-oriented teachers approach writing with such specificity that their students spend more time on their writing without being urged to do so. Paradoxically, although product oriented teachers commonly suggest that students spend more time on their writing, it is often to no avail.

Let us return to our examples to see how each student fared in his or her strategic efforts.

Calvin reviewed his first book report and checked to make sure that each sentence was grammatical. However, this draft involved only a single paragraph. He was not able to count notes, categories, or text generated from notes because he wrote the paper in a single draft directly from his thoughts. He spent the remainder of the week revising the report into paragraphs. He had never tried to organize his writing before, and he was challenged to find appropriate places to start new paragraphs. His partner pointed out that although he was creating paragraphs, they didn't seem to build on one another. Calvin's self-efficacy rating rose slightly to 4 because although he was not very sure that he could achieve a score of 5 (i.e., $5 - 1 = 4$), he felt he was on the road to figuring out how to put some organization into his report. He received a grade of 4 for the report because there was little coherence within the three sections he created.

Maria had an unexpectedly hard time applying her strategy. Her six meager notes were just a few ideas restated several different ways, which made the paper seem factually trivial or redundant. Although she took more notes than before, her notes were not categorized or used to generate text systematically. She supplied facts from memory to support her paragraphs' main sentences, but her partner often remarked that some of the supporting facts were not much more than restatements of the topic sentences. She increased her revisions (10), but most changes did little to enhance the informativeness of her prose. Maria's self-efficacy rating dropped to a realistic 7, indicating she was not sure of attaining an 8 (i.e., $8 - 1 = 7$). She finally understood what had led teachers to comment on the superficiality of her reports. Her second report earned her a 7 because the content was still somewhat shallow despite the inclusion of some interesting facts in the report.

STRATEGIC-OUTCOME MONITORING

During the following weeks, students will alter their approaches. In so doing, they will develop a repertoire of strategies that they can adjust to different writing assignments they encounter. Some students, such as Calvin, need to develop strategies because they do not achieve the outcomes that they are pursuing. Other students, such as Maria, find that their strategies are effective but insufficient for optimal achievement.

Calvin's goal of improving his book report by organizing it into three paragraphs continued to elude him. He tried to add sentences within the report that would introduce the new paragraph, but those attempts also failed. By the third day of class, Calvin consulted his teacher as well as his partner. His teacher cautioned him not to adjust his strategy haphazardly but to continue to apply it as systematically as he could. Calvin tried 30 revisions over the course of the week, but he did not make notes, organize them into categories, or generate text from them. Instead he continued to write the paper in a single draft directly from his thoughts. His self-efficacy remained at 4 because the feedback he received from his partner indicated that he was not improving the organization very much. This feedback proved correct when the report earned another grade of 4.

The following week, Calvin's partner recommended that if he wanted to organize his book report better, he might have to refine his strategy to make sure that each sentence really belonged in the paragraph in which it was located. He could do this by identifying the meaning of each sentence and then reorganizing related sentences into distinct paragraphs. Prior to attempting his third report, Calvin categorized each sentence in his second report and found that, in fact, many ideas did not belong together. He discovered that he had created paragraphs of heterogeneous sentences. He wrote the first draft of his third report in one sitting, then categorized each of its sentences, and finally reorganized the grouped sentences into paragraphs. For the first time, Calvin realized that each sentence of his report represented a separate note. He counted 40 notes in his report, which he divided into 10 categories, and he generated 10 paragraphs—one for each of the categories. Then he made about two revisions per paragraph to reorder some of the sentences. Calvin's self-efficacy rose to 6 with this effort because he was quite sure that creating categories would improve the organization of the report enough to earn him a grade of 6 (i.e., $6 + 0 = 6$). The report earned him a 7 because the content of his paper became clearer as its organization improved.

For his fifth report, Calvin adjusted his strategy further. Some of the paragraphs in his last report had been formed with just a single sentence. He decided to remove miscellaneous ideas by reworking the sentences that didn't seem to fit with any of the other sentences. His strategy was to change sentences that stood alone (so that they could be incorporated into other paragraphs) and to delete them if that was not possible. Calvin's efforts entailed twice the number of revisions as the previous week. Previously, he had never thought of writing in such a detailed way; the processes had always seemed to escape him. (Figure 12 presents Calvin's first draft of this report on the book *The Ear, the Eye, and the Arm* [Farmer, 1994]. Figure 13 shows Calvin's categorization of the sentences in his first draft. Figure 14 shows Calvin's final draft.) His self-efficacy, reflecting a cautious confidence that he might even raise his score further, was 7 (i.e., $7 + 0 = 7$). In fact, his score rose to an 8. Calvin could not remember ever having made such progress in his writing. Table 8 shows the processes involved as Calvin improved his writing skills.

Maria put greater effort into adding facts to her paragraphs. She recorded more notes and revisions but still didn't catego-

The Ear, the Eye, and the Arm
By
Nancy Farmer

This is a futuristic detective story that takes place in Africa. There are three detectives that each have different characteristics, the Ear the Eye and the Arm. The badguys are the Masks, who are a gang of headhunters who hang out in subway stations in the Cowguts, which is a cheap part of town where the detectives and other people who don't have much money can hang out. The Cowguts is in Zimbabwe. The story takes place in the year 2194. There are also a lot of fancy places like a revolving restaurant, very high in the sky, and flying buses. They also have strange things like blue monkeys that talk. The story is about how 3 kids who are children of General Matsika are kidnapped and General

Figure 12 *The first page of Calvin's first draft of his final book report.*

futuristic detective — introduction
three detectives — characters
bad guys — characters
cowguts — setting
2194 — setting
restaurant — setting
blue monkey — character
story — story
Arm — character
Ear — character
Eye — character
she Elephant — character
fight Masks — story
strange adventures — conclusion

Figure 13 *Calvin's categorization of the sentences in the first draft of his final book report.*

rize them or generate text directly from the categories. Her partner still found problems with the depth of her writing and pointed out that although Maria had 10 notes in the entire book report, they weren't grouped together. Because of this disappointing feedback, her self-efficacy remained at 7 (i.e., $7 + 0 = 7$). Although she could now see more specifically how her writing needed to improve, her grade for this third effort remained constant at 7.

Maria realized that she needed to try a new approach if she wanted to increase the content in her fourth report. This time she systematically took notes from the book,

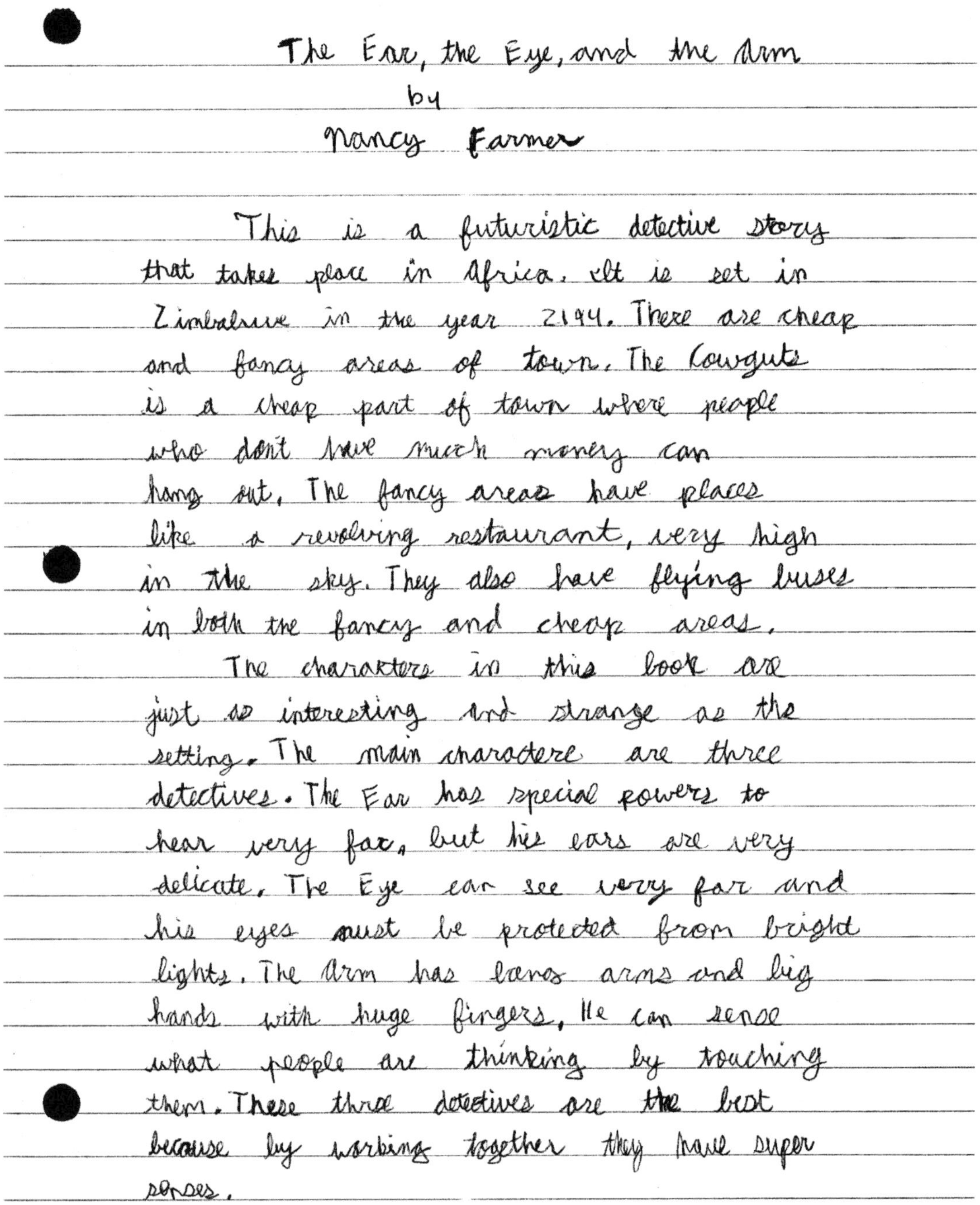

The Ear, the Eye, and the Arm
by
Nancy Farmer

This is a futuristic detective story that takes place in Africa. It is set in Zimbabwe in the year 2194. There are cheap and fancy areas of town. The Cowguts is a cheap part of town where people who don't have much money can hang out. The fancy areas have places like a revolving restaurant, very high in the sky. They also have flying buses in both the fancy and cheap areas.

The characters in this book are just as interesting and strange as the setting. The main characters are three detectives. The Ear has special powers to hear very far, but his ears are very delicate. The Eye can see very far and his eyes must be protected from bright lights. The Arm has long arms and big hands with huge fingers. He can sense what people are thinking by touching them. These three detectives are the best because by working together they have super senses.

Figure 14 *The first page of Calvin's revised draft of his final book report.*

	Assignment	Process/feedback/plan
Self-evaluation and monitoring	1	*Processes monitored*: Time = 1 hour on 1 day, notes = 0, categories = 0, generated text = 0, revisions = 0 *Feedback*: Report = 3, self-efficacy = 4
Planning and goal setting		*Goal*: Divide the draft into at least 3 paragraphs *Strategy*: Write a draft earlier in the week and get peer feedback before making a final revision.
Strategy implementation and monitoring	2	*Processes monitored*: Time = 1 hour on 1 day, 30 minutes on 3 days, notes = 0, categories = 0, generated text = 0, revisions = 25 *Feedback*: Report = 4, self-efficacy = 4
Strategic-outcome monitoring	3	*Processes monitored*: Time = 1 hour on 1 day, 30 minutes on 3 days, notes = 0, categories = 0, generated text = 0, revisions = 30 *Feedback*: Report = 4, self-efficacy = 4 *New goal*: Make sure that each paragraph contains related sentences *New strategy*: Identify what each sentence in each paragraph is about, then reorganize related sentences into distinct paragraphs
	4	*Processes monitored*: Time = 1 hour on 1 day, 30 minutes on 3 days, notes = 40, categories = 10, generated text = 10, revisions = 20 *Feedback*: Report = 7, self-efficacy = 6 *New goal*: Remove miscellaneous ideas *New strategy*: Take paragraphs composed of only a single sentence, change sentence to incorporate it into another paragraph, or delete the sentence
	5	*Processes monitored*: Time = 1 hour on 1 day, 45 minutes on 3 days, notes = 40, categories = 10, generated text = 10, revisions = 40 *Feedback*: Report = 8, self-efficacy = 7

Table 8   Calvin's Self-Regulated Development of Writing Skills

grouped the notes into categories, and then used the categories to generate text. Categories with fewer than three notes were either eliminated or supplemented with notes gained from further reading. She spent the next night generating clear and well-written paragraphs from the cate-

Table 9		Maria's Self-Regulated Development of Writing Skills
	Assignment	Process/feedback/plan
Self-evaluation and monitoring	1	*Processes monitored*: Time = 30 minutes each for 4 days, notes = 3, categories = 0, generated text = 0, revisions = 5 *Feedback*: Report = 6, self-efficacy = 9
Planning and goal setting		*Goal*: Make sure each paragraph has a single purpose *Strategy*: Combine notes so that each paragraph contains at least three supporting ideas
Strategy implementation and monitoring	2	*Processes monitored*: Time = 45 minutes each for 4 days, notes = 6, categories = 0, generated text = 0, revisions = 10 *Feedback*: Report = 7, self-efficacy = 7
Strategic-outcome monitoring	3	*Processes monitored*: Time = 45 minutes each for 4 days, notes = 10, categories = 0, generated text = 0, revisions = 20 *Feedback*: Report = 7, self-efficacy = 7 *New strategy*: Write notes from book, categorize them, generate text from the categories, and revise until the prose is polished.
	4	*Processes monitored*: Time = 1 hour each for 4 days, notes = 50, categories = 10, generated text = 10, revisions = 20 *Feedback*: Report = 10, self-efficacy = 9
	5	*Processes monitored*: Time = 90 minutes each for 4 days, notes = 50, categories = 10, generated text = 10, revisions = 40 *Feedback*: Report = 10, self-efficacy = 10

gories. She called her partner to get feedback regarding her draft of the book report. For the first time in memory, she received comments indicating that not only was her report well written but it was also rich with ideas. Her teacher agreed and awarded Maria the 10 she had sought. Her self-efficacy reflected her increased capability, rising to 9, which she was quite sure of attaining (i.e., $9 = 0 = 9$). Table 9 shows the processes involved as Maria improved her writing taking skills.

Calvin's and Maria's case studies show that by attending to specific details of the processes they used to produce their reports, they each found a unique way to address their deficits and to build on their strengths. Their results demonstrate how self-regulatory methods help students who differ widely in achievement develop their skills.

SELF-EFFICACY PERCEPTIONS

A lack of improvement in self-efficacy following strategy implementation is far from catastrophic. In contrast, it is an opportunity for students to develop further their self-regulatory skills. Through accurate self-monitoring, students can ferret out unproductive strategies and devise successful ones. They will discover that self-regulated learning is not a magic wand that produces effortless results but rather it requires exertion. However, the resulting increases in one's command of both subject matter and the process of learning is gratifying. As students perfect their self-regulatory skills, they acquire confidence in their methods and ability to learn.

> Students' failure to produce gains in efficacy can be a valuable indicator of either an incorrect strategy choice or a breakdown in strategy implementation.

Students' initial self-efficacy perceptions are often inflated, as was the case with Maria. But as youngsters monitor and self-record their efforts to learn, they must confront a different reality that compels them to adjust their self-efficacy perceptions. When this occurs, self-efficacy judgments become a powerful tool for discerning how to improve their strategic efforts.

To assist implementing this self-regulatory cycle for students' writing, we have provided a checklist in Exhibit 13.

EXHIBIT 13 | **Teacher's Checklist for Developing Students' Writing Skills**

1. Planning
   ___ Plan writing activities (See Implementation, below) lasting 5 weeks so that they mesh coherently with the curriculum
   ___ Make sure that writing assignments are equal in length and difficulty
2. Implementation
   ___ Introduce concept of self-efficacy and how to calculate it
   ___ Prepare adequate supply of a writing chart similar to that shown in Exhibit 12
   ___ Model use of the writing chart
   ___ Prepare and administer writing assignments over 5 weeks to provide adequate feedback to students on the effectiveness of their strategy use
   ___ Prepare and model draft processes, including raw notes, categorized notes, beginning draft of text, and revisions
   ___ Provide small or peer group time in class to permit students to evaluate together their own and others' writing skills and to refine them (weekly)
   ___ Observe small or peer groups to obtain insights into which writing strategies work and why (weekly)
   ___ Use information gathered from observing groups as a springboard for brief whole-class discussions on strategy selection and refinement (weekly)
   ___ Keep records of students' writing chart (including self-efficacy) scores
   ___ Determine whether there is congruence between self-efficacy and other writing chart scores for each student. If not, data may indicate the need for teacher's attention to "stand out" students (either overly high or low in perceived self-efficacy, given other writing chart results)
3. Follow-up
   ___ Plan and implement writing follow-up activities for some time later in the course (to reinforce prior writing skills) deficiency, such as poor weekly quiz performance. A teacher can help a student pinpoint problems underlying his or her academic work and self-monitor key aspects of his or her studying

1 In which aspects of writing will your students need the most help?

2 Which sections of the Writing Self-Monitoring Form will be most helpful for your students? Are there any sections of the form you might you wish to change, and if so, how they could be adapted?

3 What problems do you anticipate in helping your students self-monitor their writing?

4 Describe the writing strategies that will be most helpful to your students and explain why the strategies could help.

SUGGESTED READINGS

El-Dinary, Brown, R., & Van Meter, P. (1995). Strategy instruction for improving writing. In E. Wood, V.E. Woloshyn, & T. Willoughby (Eds.), *Cognitive strategy instruction for middle and high schools* (pp. 88–116). Cambridge, MA: Brookline Books.

Harris, K.R., & Graham, S. (1992). *Helping young readers master the craft: Strategy instruction and self-regulation of the writing process.* Cambridge, MA: Brookline Books.

Pressley, M., McGoldrick J.A., Cariglia-Bull, T., & Symons, S. (1995). Writing. In M. Pressley, V. Woloshyn, J. Burkell, T. Cariglia-Bull, L. Lysynchuk, J.A. McGoldrick, B. Schneider, B.L. Snyder, & S. Symons (Eds.), *Cognitive strategy instruction that really improves children's academic performance* (2nd ed., pp. 153–183). Cambridge, MA: Brookline Books.

Scardamalia, M., & Bereiter, C. (1986). Research on written composition. In M. C. Wittrock (Ed.), *Handbook of research on teaching* (3rd ed., pp. 778–803). New York: Macmillan.

final issues

Introducing Self-Regulated
Learning Into the Classroom

Teaching self-regulation to others requires a sense of humility about knowing what it takes for another person to learn, because academic learning, like other forms of learning, is ultimately a personal experience.

Developing a self-regulatory level of study skills with students as diverse as Calvin and Maria depends greatly on the capabilities, enthusiasm, and perspectives of their teachers. Teachers cannot give students an expert's understanding and skill, but they can provide the self-regulatory tools to discover what works best for the student themselves. For this reason, we believe that teachers are most effective when they function as models, consultants, and coaches, such as in an academy. Teachers can provide students with strategies and show them how to self-monitor their own learning processes accurately and accept the outcomes positively. Teachers are most effective when they model a positive self-efficacy perspective about the power of self-regulated learning processes for each of their students. Let's consider some of these key teaching capabilities in more detail.

KEY INSTRUCTIONAL CAPABILITIES

To bring a self-regulated learning model to life in classrooms, teachers must be capable of (a) demonstrating use of various self-regulated learning techniques, (b) demonstrating the effectiveness of self-regulatory techniques in ways that students will understand and accept, (c) keeping records of students' progress, (d) anticipating students' questions regarding self-regulated learning, (e) planning for the integration of self-regulated processes within the curriculum, and (f) refining their own planning and teaching methods in light of their experience with self-regulation training.

Let us consider each of these six essential capabilities of teachers who have successfully implemented self-regulatory training into the curriculum of their classes.

1. *Demonstrating use of various self-regulated learning techniques.* From a social learning perspective, teachers must be able to model and describe the use of self-regulated learning techniques to their students. These instructors must also display a firm commitment to implementing self-regulated learning in their classrooms if students are to be motivated to adopt them as well. This is

essential because it takes additional planning and multiple efforts to implement self-regulatory techniques, such as goal setting and self-recording, and some students may be reluctant to try these methods without strong teacher support. Finally, teachers need to generalize from the observed examples of self-regulation and show students how self-regulatory techniques can be adapted to meet their own individual goals and style of learning.

2. *Demonstrating the effectiveness of self-regulatory techniques.* Teachers must be able to show and explain the outcomes of self-regulatory techniques. For some students, the effectiveness of self-regulation techniques will be easily observed, but for others, it will not. Teachers need to be sensitive to differences in students' awareness of how self-regulatory techniques work and how to self-evaluate their usefulness during studying. Assisting students to appropriately identify and self-evaluate learning outcomes requires patience and empathy because students vary considerably in their background and prior training.

3. *Keeping records of students' progress.* Some teachers will find that recording their students' progress in becoming self-regulative an easy addition to the other records they normally collect, but other teachers will see any increase in record keeping as a burdensome demand on their scarce time. However, such records are essential for high-quality supervision of students' self-regulatory development. We have found that keeping records of students' self-regulatory processes can be designed to be minimally burdensome if teachers simplify the forms and involve students in the process. As we noted earlier, it is important to check students' evaluations of their peers to ensure the accuracy of their judgmental criteria.

For statistically disinclined teachers, the great bulk of students' performance monitoring can be shifted to the students themselves by asking them to hand in self-recorded data or graphs on particular performance dimensions. Students can be asked to keep their records as part of a personal portfolio marking their progress as self-regulated learners. Such portfolios can involve graphed summaries of personal and class outcomes constructed by the students; these summary analyses help students become more aware of strategic causes of their successes and can motivate them toward skill attainment. The teachers' primary role will be to discern trends and provide advice regarding student-produced data.

For statistically inclined (and equipped) teachers, electronic grading programs designed for personal computers may be used to record various exercise scores and to compute class and individual means. Plotting of class and individual means over time by using graphing programs will reveal progress toward greater self-regulatory skill or self-efficacy. Robert Kovach has found that sharing of plotted group outcomes can be a springboard for class discussion of personal strategy choices as well as classwide improvements in self-regulation. Here, too, the role of the teacher is primarily to pinpoint individual or group deficiencies and to help students refine their techniques and strategies. For both statistically inclined and disinclined teachers, the burden of record keeping should be shifted as much as possible to students because ultimately they will need to gather and interpret this information on their own.

4. *Anticipating students' questions regarding self-regulated learning.* Some students react to changes in classroom procedures and expectations with uncertainty or anxiety. Even those students who understand and accept self-regulated learning intuitively may have questions regarding their teacher's expectations, such as the following: "Why do we have to do this, especially since I am a good student already?" "Are we going to be graded on this?" "How can you grade how we study?" "What do these skills have to do with learning the subject?" "If I don't progress as fast or as far as my classmates, will my grade be affected?" "Why do I have to help a classmate? That's the teacher's job." "Won't working on skills take time away from the curriculum?" It is important that teachers anticipate these and similar questions to answer them in ways that are convincing and reassuring. Regarding the first question, for example, teachers could mention that *all* students need to improve their study skills to succeed with more difficult assignments, during subsequent courses, and more advanced schools, such as high school and college.

Furthermore, teachers must set forth a clear policy regarding the need for students to implement and self-record their self-regulatory activities during homework and the consequences of noncompliance, such as missed assignment marks or unfavorable grades. At the collegiate level, faculty (Weinstein, Stone, & Hanson, 1993) have reported that grading students' efforts to self-regulate was essential to ensure high-quality implementation. Some students will not invest the time to become self-regulatory without some sort of academic contingency; once they become aware of the effectiveness of these techniques, however, their self-efficacy perceptions will increase along with their intrinsic motivation to continue to use these methods. These self-growth dynamics are highlighted in a learning academy setting that frees the teacher to function as a supportive coach.

5. *Planning for the integration of self-regulated learning processes within the curriculum.* Careful planning of self-regulatory instruction, which is no more difficult than planning additional content components, is essential to ensure proper implementation. At least five facets of planning need to be considered when teaching self-regulated learning as part of the curriculum: (a) adequacy of lead time for presenting each cyclic self-regulatory step in learning the five academic study skills; (b) optimal course layout (i.e., decisions as to where and when in the regular course schedule to introduce and extend self-regulatory skills), (c) consistent difficulty in self-regulatory assignments so that students can self-evaluate their progress against similar task "loads"; (d) continued use of skills throughout the curriculum rather than developing a skill and then leaving it to chance for further use and refinement (systematic reuse of the skills is crucial to additional learning and to transfer to new contexts, and it demonstrates the usefulness of a given skill across a variety of tasks and engenders a sense of personal mastery); and (e) no appearance of a dichotomy between self-regulatory "process" and learning "content." It is our view that mastery of learning skills is crucial to an in-depth grasp of course content.

6. *Refining planning and teaching methods in light of self-regulation training experiences.* As we noted earlier, self-regulating learning is an inherently cyclic process because strategic methods must be adjusted continually to chang-

ing conditions. This same principle is as true for teaching self-regulatory methods as it is for learning to use them. Teachers should not assume that their first attempt to teach a student or a class of students a self-regulatory technique will be effective. At best, an instructor's initial effort will be an approximation that must be refined on the basis of students' verbal and performance feedback. Just as students need practice in learning self-regulatory skills, so too will instructors need to reflect on outcomes of initial efforts and to redraft their teaching methods in light of these self-evaluations.

In conclusion, these six essential instructional capabilities, ranging from self-regulatory modeling to reflective self-evaluation, enable a teacher to successfully implement self-regulatory training in the curriculum of their classes. For teachers who have concerns about the effectiveness or feasibility of incorporating these procedures, we recommend starting with time management because students readily see its importance and self-monitoring is relatively easy for students. These teachers may wish to focus on this module until they feel comfortable with the self-regulatory cycle and then proceed with the next most comfortable learning skill. In addition, some teachers may wish to observe other teachers who have already implemented such modules.

THE PARENTS' ROLE

Several specific points need to be emphasized to parents. First, even *A* students waste study time, read and take notes

> These study skills are useful for all students, not just those experiencing academic difficulties.

inefficiently, need to improve their writing, and often prepare for tests haphazardly. Most students are not systematic about their studying and often rely on idiosyncratic methods that they devised over the years. Self-regulatory training will make them more aware of their strengths as well as their limitations, and it will show them how to determine whether a new learning strategy really makes a difference for them.

Second, parents should be told how self-monitoring and recording will better assist their youngsters to self-observe and self-evaluate their learning. If they are not briefed ahead of time, some parents may see self-recording as unnecessary busy work that could detract from course-content mastery.

Third, parents should be encouraged to help set aside a regularly scheduled time during which their children can do their homework and self-recording. When parents see study skills as an advantage in attaining their youngsters' future academic goals, they will be more willing to cooperate in setting up conducive studying conditions at home.

Fourth, if parents usually help their children during studying, they may want to learn more about the effectiveness of various learning strategies. Such parents typically rely on learning techniques that worked for them as students, and they can benefit from observing methods that have been scientifically validated.

Finally, parents should be alerted to watch for signs of growth in their children's studying and to praise them for small improvements in skill. Parental support for their children's academic self-regulatory development is essential for the youngsters' valuing and internalization of these skills.

INVESTMENT IN SELF-REGULATED LEARNING

Instruction in self-regulation processes is an investment in student growth that holds the promise of short-, intermediate-, and long-term returns. In a word, the benefits of self-regulatory training relate to students' *growth*. As they grasp and refine the capability to self-regulate their learning, they can be expected to grow in three major ways: (a) in their understanding of subject matter content, (b) in their learning efficiency, and (c) in their perceived self-efficacy for accomplishing additional learning tasks.

> An instructors' investment in self-regulatory skill training will yield numerous dividends throughout a course and beyond.

The positive effects of students' self-regulation are not limited to homework assignments and test-taking experiences; there are classroom benefits as well. For example, improved student participation throughout the course because fewer of them report being "lost." With increased participation, teachers will also enjoy an improved quality of discussion and a more infectious sense of class interest in the topic. With these benefits, another naturally follows: Fewer students need to be closely regimented and "rescued" from failing. Thus, the teacher should experience less end-of-term pressure to find a way for marginal students to pass.

> The effects of self-regulatory training can raise the morale of both students and teachers.

Improvement in students' morale is a natural product of their increased understanding, engagement, and perceived self-efficacy; an increase in the teacher's morale stems from watching students grow in self-confidence as they discover ways of learning that really work. Finally, self-regulatory training will improve the students' academic test performance, which is often, unfortunately, interpreted as a measure of teacher effectiveness. Thus, under the self-regulation model of learning, teachers are empowered as well as students.

CONCLUSION

No learning technique or strategy is universally effective, and thus we must constantly self-evaluate our effectiveness as learners to optimally refine our strategic approaches. We especially need these powerful learning techniques when the academic going gets tough—for passing intimidating examinations, for making sense of confusing lectures or poorly written text material, for using insufficient preparation time effectively, and for pleasing demanding literary critics. As students move through the educational system from elementary school to college, more choices and freedom are offered and more self-regulation is expected of them, but available information suggests that students' studying and degree of self-reliance does not increase correspondingly.

> The development of self-regulatory skill is a lifelong pursuit for all of us.

From the perceptive of the teacher, students who take responsibility for their learning are more enjoyable to teach. Self-regulated students view their teachers more as resources and less as threatening figures. Teachers can transform their classrooms into learning academies by following the guidelines for teaching the various learning skills contained in this book. Students who attend such a learning academy will gain something more valuable than merely an appreciation of the importance of content matter; they will take with them a broad repertoire of study strategies, the self-regulatory capacity to apply and refine the strategies on their own, and the sense of self-efficacy to accept academic work as a personal challenge.

glossary

Cyclic model of self-regulated learning—a learning model characterized by the four phases of: (a) self-monitoring and evaluation, (b) planning and goal setting, (c) strategy implementation and monitoring, (d) and strategic-outcome monitoring.

Deliberate practice—specific goal-directed practice episodes involving tasks structured to provide interpretable feedback, such as using flash cards to learn foreign words.

Feedback—information derived about performance from knowledgeable peers, teachers, or self-evaluation, such as effectiveness data.

Goal Setting—committing oneself to specific, proximal, and challenging learning outcomes, such as getting an *A* in a course.

Learning academy—a form of school designed to improve performance as well as impart established knowledge through expert and peer modeling, direct social feedback for performance efforts, and practice routines involving specific goals and methods of self-monitoring.

Learning processes—methods by which students learn, such as selective reading, systematic note taking, study time planning and management, and test anticipation and preparation.

Learning outcomes—results or products of learning, such as recall and comprehension of academic content matter.

Modeling—teaching through demonstration and explanation, such as showing how to solve a mathematics problem in stepwise fashion and encouraging student imitation.

Proto-exams—tests that mimic the form and time lag of real exams but cover material assigned over a 2-week period.

Reactive effects—cognitive and emotional reactions to self-monitored outcomes of one's learning, such as heightened attention following a failure.

Record-keeping—the transcribing of data regarding one's functioning at a skilled task, such as recording the time used to complete homework assignments.

Reiterative learning—learning that takes place over several cycles (or attempts) in which fresh feedback on performance is used to refine goals and strategies, such as successively modifying one's writing strategy to improve a paper.

Self-efficacy—the degree to which a person feels capable of successfully performing a certain task, such as solving a type of science problem.

Self-evaluation—occurs when students judge their personal effectiveness, often from observations and recordings of prior performances and outcomes.

Self-monitoring—systematic, deliberate observation of covert and overt aspects of one's performance on a given task, such as reading comprehension.

Self-regulation—self-generated thoughts, feelings, and actions that are directed toward attainment of one's education goals.

Self-regulated learning—an approach to learning involving goal setting, strategy use, self-monitoring, and self-adjustment to acquire a skill, such as improved vocabulary.

Smart learner—a student who uses self-regulatory processes to learn more efficiently and effectively.

Strategic planning—deciding on which strategy or component of a strategy to implement during the next performance or study effort.

Strategies—cognitive procedures that students can use to help them understand tasks and perform actions to attain a goal.

Strategy refinement—discovering which features of a given strategy produce selected aspects of the outcomes.

Task analysis—breaking a task into component parts to facilitate its learning, such as breaking reading comprehension into finding the main ideas and summarizing.

references

American 2000: An Education Strategy. (1990). Washington, DC: U.S. Department of Education.

Bandura, A. (1986). *Social foundations of thought and action: A social cognitive theory.* Englewood Cliffs, NJ: Prentice-Hall.

Butler, D. L., & Winne, P. H. (1995). Feedback and self-regulated learning: A theoretical synthesis. *Review of Educational Research, 65,* 245–281.

DeWitt, K. (1992, April 16). Survey shows U.S. children write seldom and not well. *The New York Times,* p. A-1.

Ellis, D. (1994). *Becoming a master student.* Rapid City, SD: College Survival.

Ericsson, K. A., & Charness, N. (1994). Expert performance: Its structure and acquisition. *American Psychologist, 49,* 725–747.

Farmer, N. (1994). *The ear, the eye, and the arm.* New York: Scholastic.

Ghatala, E. S., Levin, J. R., Foorman, B. R., & Pressley, M. (1989). Improving children's regulation of their reading PREP time. *Contemporary Educational Psychology, 14,* 49–66.

Kozol, J. (1985). *Illiterate American.* Garden City, NY: Anchor Press/Doubleday.

Newman, R. S. (1994). Academic help-seeking: A strategy of self-regulated learning. In D. H. Schunk & B. J. Zimmerman (Eds.), *Self-regulation of learning and performance: Issues and educational applications* (pp. 283–301). Hillsdale, NJ: Erlbaum.

Pintrich, P. R., & DeGroot, E. V. (1990). Motivational and self-regulated learning components of classroom academic performance. *Journal of Educational Psychology, 82,* 33–40.

Pressley, M., Woloshyn, V., Burkell, J., Cariglia-Bull, T., Lysynchuk, L., McGoldrick, J. A., Schneider, B., Snyder, B. L., & Symons, S. (1995). *Cognitive strategy instruction that really improves children's academic performance* (2nd ed.). Cambridge, MA: Brookline Books.

Schunk, D. H., & Swartz, C. W. (1993). Goals and progress feedback: Effects on self-efficacy and writing achievement. *Contemporary Educational Psychology, 18,* 337–354.

Schunk, D. H., & Zimmerman, B. J. (Eds.). (1994). *Self-regulation of learning and performance: Issues and educational applications.* Hillsdale, NJ: Erlbaum.

Schunk, D. H., & Zimmerman, B. J. (1996). Modeling and self-efficacy influences on children's development of self-regulation. In K. Wentzel & J. Juvonen (Eds.), *Social motivation: Understanding children's school adjustment* (pp. 154–180). New York: Cambridge University Press.

Stevenson, R. L. (1986). *Treasure island.* Cranford, NJ: Dylithium.

Weinstein, C. E., Stone, G., & Hanson, G. (1993). *The long-term effects of a strategic learning course for college students.* Unpublished manuscript, University of Texas, Austin.

Wood, E., Woloshyn, V. E., & Willoughby, T. (1995). *Cognitive strategy instruction for middle and high schools.* Cambridge, MA: Bookline Books.

Zimmerman, B. J. (1985). The development of "intrinsic" motivation: A social learning analysis. In G. J. Whitehurst (Ed.), *Annals of child development* (pp. 117–160). Greenwich, CT: JAI Press.

Zimmerman, B. J. (1989). A social cognitive view of self-regulated academic learning. *Journal of Educational Psychology, 81*(3), 329–339.

Zimmerman, B. J. (1995). Self-efficacy and educational development. In A. Bandura (ed.), *Self-efficacy in changing societies* (pp. 202–231). New York: Cambridge University Press.

Zimmerman, B. J., & Bandura, A. (1994). Impact of self-regulatory influences on attainment in a writing course. *American Educational Research Journal, 29,* 663–676.

Zimmerman, B. J., Bandura, A., & Martinez-Pons, M. (1992). Self-motivation for academic attainment: The role of self-efficacy beliefs and personal goal setting. *American Educational Research Journal, 29,* 663–676.

Zimmerman, B. J., Greenberg, D., & Weinstein, C. E. (1994). Self-regulating academic study time: A strategy approach. In D. H. Schunk & B. J. Zimmerman (Ed.), *Self-*

regulation of learning and performance: Issues and educational applications (pp. 181–199). Hillsdale, NJ: Erlbaum.

Zimmerman, B. J., & Martinez-Pons, M. (1986). Development of a structured interview for assessing student use of self-regulated learning strategies. *American Educational Research Journal, 23*(4), 614–628.

Zimmerman, B. J., & Martinez-Pons, M. (1988). Construct validation of a strategy model of student self-regulated learning. *Journal of Educational Psychology, 80*(3), 284–290.

Zimmerman, B. J., & Martinez-Pons, M. (1990). Student differences in self-regulated learning: Relating grade, sex, and giftedness to self-efficacy and strategy use. *Journal of Educational Psychology, 82*(1), 51–59.

Zimmerman, B. J., & Paulsen, A. S. (1995) Self-monitoring during collegiate studying: An invaluable tool for academic self-regulation. In P. Pintrich (Ed.), *New directions in college teaching and learning* (Vol. 63, pp. 13–27). San Francisco, Jossey-Bass.

Zimmerman, B. J., & Schunk, D. E. (Eds.). (1989). *Self-regulated learning and academic achievement: Theory, research, and practice.* New York: Springer-Verlag.

ABOUT THE AUTHORS

Barry J. Zimmerman is a Distinguished Professor of Educational Psychology at the Graduate School and University Center of City University of New York and Head of the Learning, Development, and Instruction subarea. He is the President of Division 15 of the American Psychological Association and has received the Division 16 Senior Scientist Award for lifetime contributions in 1994. He has published more than 100 articles and chapters on learning and motivational processes of children and youth from a social cognitive perspective. He has authored or edited six books, including two on the topic of self-regulated learning and its development.

Sebastian Bonner is an advanced degree candidate in Educational Psychology at the Graduate School and University Center of the City University of New York. He is presently conducting research on how self-regulatory skills develop among elementary and intermediate school children. Mr. Bonner has taught courses at the high school and college levels in New York City. His first experience in teaching was gained in Taiwan, where he taught adult education courses and conducted corporate education seminars.

Robert Kovach has taught social studies for more than two decades at Paul D. Schreiber High School in Port Washington, NY, which was recognized by the Department of Education as among the most outstanding high schools in the United States. He has developed a variety of innovative procedures for assessing his students' self-regulated methods of learning, their understanding of the effectiveness of those methods, and their beliefs about themselves as learners. He has a master's degree in teaching from the University of Wisconsin at River Falls and is a PhD candidate at the Graduate School and University Center of the City University of New York.

Correspondence concerning this book should be addressed to Barry J. Zimmerman, Educational Psychology Program, CUNY Graduate Center, 33 West 42nd Street, New York, NY 10036-8099.

Jefferson College Library
Hillsboro, MO 63050